The Particular Nature of
Freemasonry

by Michael R. Poll

A Cornerstone Book

The Particular Nature of Freemasonry
by Michael R. Poll

A Cornerstone Book
Published by Cornerstone Book Publishers
Copyright © 2020 by Michael R. Poll

All rights reserved under International and Pan-American Copyright Conventions. No part of this book may be reproduced in any manner without permission in writing from the copyright holder, except by a reviewer, who may quote brief passages in a review.

Cornerstone Book Publishers
New Orleans, LA
www.cornerstonepublishers.com

First Cornerstone Edition – 2020

ISBN: 978-1-887560-37-5

Table of Contents

Introduction vii
Our Changing Freemasonry 1
My Brother's Keeper 17
What Does it Mean to be Irregular? 23
What is Masonic Education? 33
Freemasonry During the COVID-19 Pandemic 39
Forgotten Symbolism of the Festive Board 43
Is Freemasonry a Moral Philosophy? 53
Is it OK to Laugh? 57
Forbidden Subjects in Lodge 59
How (and will) You be Remembered? 63
The Reality of Masonic Education 67
Just What is Important in Freemasonry? 75
The Five to Ten Minute Masonic Lecture 79
Scottish Rite Questions and Answers 85
"We Meet Upon the Level" 95
Should Masons be Allowed to Smoke,
Eat, or Drink in Open Lodge? 99
Masonic Dirty Laundry 105
Do We Need Masonic Charity? 109
A Growing Danger for Freemasonry 115
How Important is a Mason's Reputation? 123
Balancing Masonry in Our Lives 135
About The Author 142

Introduction

Legend tells us that Christianity was brought into Armenia in the first century AD by the apostles Thaddeus and Bartholomew.[1] We can only guess at what these apostles taught the Armenians as the Armenians developed a unique version of Christianity that differed from the teachings of Orthodox or Byzantine Christianity. Over time, the Armenian Church firmly claimed to be Christian, but the differences between their version of Christianity and the already established Church became significant. To highlight some of these differences, the Armenians rejected the Fourth Ecumenical Council in 451 AD, which was recognized by the Patriarch of Constantinople and the Pope in Rome.[2] The Armenians had their form of Christianity and desired to keep it as they liked. Today, this is not so uncommon as the many Protestant faiths differ slightly to widely from the Catholic Church in more than a few areas. But it is interesting that such differences in religion could exist in these early times. Logic would dictate that the differences came from either a lack of proper education when the religion was first introduced or a desire to edit what was taught after the apostles left.

Freemasonry is today facing something of a similar situation as the Armenian Church. Proper Masonic education was absent for too many years in too many lodges. Masons began defining Masonic teachings, principles, and laws by however they understood them. Today we are seeing examples of Masonry on all levels that differ slightly to profoundly. We are seeing differing Masonic philosophies with each boldly, and with considerable authority, claiming to be *the* correct Masonic philosophy. Not everyone can be correct. So, what exactly is Freemasonry?

It is not my goal or desire to attempt to portray *the* definitive version of Freemasonry in this book. It is only my intention to offer the results of my study of classic Masonic educational writings along with observations of the world around us. The hope is to generate some thought and dialogue between Masons on the nature of Freemasonry. I have tried to look at Masonry today and how we have taught in the past. I have tried to reconcile the two into a plan of action for Masons and lodges.

This book is offered with a desire to be of service to Freemasonry. We are in a time of great change. The hope is that this may generate a bit of light into dark corners. '

Michael R. Poll
Spring, 2020

Notes:

1. https://armeniadiscovery.com/en/articles/religion-in-armenia.
2. https://www.ancient.eu/article/1253/the-differences-between-byzantine--armenian-christ/.

The Particular Nature of Freemasonry

Our Changing Freemasonry

Over the last few years, I've received a good many e-mails from Masons in different U.S. jurisdictions. Regardless of where the mails come from, many seem to have a common theme. They basically say, "I am not happy" and then when they give the reason as to why they are not happy, it has something to do with some aspect of change. But the Masons are not all in agreement as to the deeper problems that are creating the changes. It is here that divisions begin.

One group of the disgruntled is mostly composed of, but not all, younger Masons. They point at the older Masons and say that *they* are the source of the problems. *"It's those old guys! They refuse to change! All they want out of Freemasonry is to read minutes and argue over bills. They want nothing else and known nothing else!"*

The other unhappy group is the older Masons. Again, not all, but mostly. They point at the young Masons and say that *they* are the problem. *"Those young kids are creating trouble! They are trying to shove new things on us that we don't understand or want. They want us to change from how we have always done things.* **They** *are the problem!"*

Two sides with firm opinions on problems along with who and what is wrong. So, which side is the right side?

To begin to understand this situation and problem, we need to first look at the concept of change itself. The truth of the matter is that it does not matter what anyone likes, dislikes, wants, or does not want. Change is going to happen. It happens every day. Our grass keeps needing cutting, our house needs to be repainted, and we get older and hurt where we never hurt before. Change is natural. It happens to everyone and everything.

And Freemasonry is constantly changing. I once heard someone say with all the authority in the world, *"Freemasonry does not change. In fact, innovations are not permitted in Masonry."* Well, that's just nonsense. Freemasonry is constantly changing. Every year resolutions are passed at Grand Lodge that change Masonry in that jurisdiction. By-laws are changed, members join and die. That's changes. Elections are held every year in lodges, Grand Lodges and other bodies which are also changes.

What is actually meant by the belief that change is not allowed is that unauthorized, or improper, changes are not allowed. For example, let's say that a Worshipful Master comes to a meeting and unexpectedly makes an announcement. Let's say that he tells the lodge that he has been thinking and decided that the lodge building is not suitable. So, on his own, he sold the building and bought another building in the lodge's name across town. He even changed the meeting date for good measure. Well, needless to say, that's an unauthorized and improper change. The Worshipful Master of a lodge does not have the authority on his own to sell or buy property for the lodge without the lodge's permission. It does not mean that it can't be done, but there is an established procedure for how the lodge can do things.

We are an organization of rules and laws. We are all bound to those rules and must follow them. Change happens all the time, but it is unauthorized changes in our rules and laws that are not allowed.

Freemasonry is also tied to society. What affects the community, affects us. In fact, I believe that changes in society in the first half of the 1900s play a role in what's happening in Freemasonry today. Let's look at just a few of those changes.

World War I certainly changed the world. While the United States was not the location of the battles, many from our military were killed and the U.S. as a country, along with the people, did suffer from this war. Once the war was over, it was not long before another period of hardship came. The economy took a strong downward turn, banks failed, the stock market crashed, and we went into a period of time known as the Great Depression.

My parents grew up during the Great Depression. They told me that during this time they were outright poor. But what they also told me was that while they were poor, they didn't really know it because everyone around them was poor. Everyone was just like them and in the same situation. The Great Depression affected most everyone and most lost pretty much everything they had in the bank failures and the general financial hardships of the time.

As the Great Depression was ending, another change took place. But this was certainly not a positive change either. Following the Great Depression came World War II.

With the exception of Pearl Harbor, the mainland of the United States was again not a battleground for the new war. But the times were still very difficult in the United States. My parents were teenagers and young adults during this time. My dad was drafted to fight in the war. Both said that even though money was generally not as tight as during the Great Depression, everything was rationed. Even if you wanted to buy things like coffee, sugar, meat, or even white dress shirts, you needed a coupon. If your allotment for anything was used up for that month, then you did without.

Sometime back, I watched a documentary about London and Berlin during World War II. Both cities were heavily bombed during the war with scars remaining from the bombings even today. London was bombed by the Germans and Berlin by the Allies. What surprised me was the number of bombs dropped. Literally thousands of bombs were dropped on just these two cities. One eyewitness account said that when the bombing started, and the bombers flew overhead, there were so many of them that they blocked out the sun. But then the war ended, and that was good. But how it ended changed the world forever.

At the close of the war, one bomber flew over the city of Hiroshima, Japan. That one bomber carried just one bomb. That one bomb destroyed the entire city. A few days later, another bomber flew over Nagasaki and again dropped just one bomb. Again, that one bomb destroyed that whole city. Never before had the world seen that much destruction power from any one weapon. Japan surrendered and the world was never the same again.

I wasn't born until after the war was over. I never lived in a nonnuclear world. But the dropping of those bombs must have changed something deep within the people living during that time. How could it not?

I won't attempt to go into the minds of anyone else, but at the close of the war there seems to have been a tremendous change in the United States. If you stop and think about it, we had a half a century of horribly difficult times. War, poverty, hunger, loss of everything. It seems that at the close of WWII, everyone just wanted to stop and take a break from trouble.

They wanted a rest, some niceness, a bit of a vacation from hardship and pain. People now had a few dollars in their pockets, and they wanted to use it in ways that created enjoyment.

My grandfather was Worshipful Master of Friends of Harmony Lodge Number 58 in New Orleans in 1945. This would become my Mother Lodge 30 years later. I used to hear stories about how Masons went to lodge during this time from my family and older Masons. Friends of Harmony along with a number of other lodges, met the old Masonic Temple Building on St. Charles Avenue in New Orleans. Lodge meeting nights were very much a family event. Entire families would gather at the temple building in the evening and go to the second floor. There was a large dining hall there with a sizeable kitchen attached to it. The families would have a nice dinner. Everyone would visit, talk of current events, and enjoy themselves. Lodge night was always a good time.

After they were finished dinner, the men would go upstairs to their lodge meeting and the wives and children would go downstairs to the basement. In the basement, there was an Olympic size swimming pool where the kids could go swimming. It was a great time for everyone. The kids would have a great time in the pool and the ladies would visit with each other. After the meeting was over, the men would go down to the swimming pool area and everyone visit for a little longer. After a time, maybe they'd go upstairs to the second floor to get a bit of dessert and a last cup of coffee. Everyone would then go home. It was always a very enjoyable evening for everyone. This was generally what was needed — a little niceness, peace, and enjoyment.

I can't tell you that this experience was a carbon copy for everyone in every lodge across the United States, but I can tell you that a very strange and unexplained change happened during this time in lodges all over. Masonic membership dramatically spiked and reached a height in numbers that had never been reached before. For reasons that have never been explained, new members came to Masonry and in numbers like never before. So many new members came that Grand lodges were forced to build, restructure, and expand to accommodate all the new members. Where once a single Grand Secretary could handle all the business matters, a staff of secretaries and workers was then needed in order to handle the ever-growing workload.

I found no reason ever given for the significant increase in members during the time following World War II, but it does seem clear that there was something in Freemasonry that appealed to many more men than previously. Maybe it was the enjoyable family atmosphere of the Masonic experience, or maybe something deeper and unexplained having to do with the nature of the rituals and symbolic ceremonies. Regardless of why, membership across the United States, and the world, increased dramatically.

If the membership in Freemasonry greatly grew because of some desire for pleasant times and family entertainment and if the Masonic experience was filling that desire, then we can see competition developing in ways like never before. An invention came during this time that again changed the world. The television set.

I remember as a young boy my parents were the first ones in our family to have a television. I well remember both sets of grandparents as well as aunts and uncles coming over to watch this great invention. It was the thing to do. Everyone was amazed. There was something sitting there in the living room that was just as good as going to the movies, actually better because you didn't have to leave your house. It was right there at home for you to watch.

Soon, the TV was on most all the time so that you could watch your favorite show. But that was not all. Before too long other inventions came along guaranteed to make life more convenient and enjoyable. A few of these inventions were directly associated with the television.

I remember when growing up there were two ways that I could get dinner. One was for my mother (or someone) to fix dinner from scratch in the kitchen. The other was to go out to a restaurant. That was it. Someone cooked dinner on the stove or we went out to a restaurant. Then one evening my mother came into the living room smiling. She announced that she was not going to fix dinner that evening. I remember thinking to myself, *okay, I guess that means we're going out to a restaurant*. But then she quickly added that we were not going out to eat. I remember being puzzled and wondering if this meant that we would go hungry that night.

My mother then pulled out several little rectangular boxes and said that we were going to have something new for dinner — TV dinners. She asked if we wanted roast beef, turkey with stuffing, or fried chicken. She then put the little trays covered with aluminum into the oven and before too long we had dinner. It was amazing.

But the inventions didn't stop with dinner. Yes, the TV dinners were great. Now, we could have dinner at home, Mom didn't have to work in the kitchen, and we could watch TV while we ate. Well, somewhat. You see the television was in the living room, and the table where we ate was in the dining room. We had to stretch our necks to watch the TV while we ate and some of us were simply not able to watch TV at all. That's where another invention, also connected to the TV, came into our lives. My dad brought home *TV trays* one day. It was great. Now, we could all sit around the TV in chairs and eat our TV dinners on small TV trays while watching our favorite TV show. TV ruled!

Soon more inventions came out to make life simpler, more convenient, and enjoyable. We didn't have to leave the house to have great entertainment. By the 1960s and early 1970s, the dramatic increase in Masonic membership peaked and memberships began to decline. Just like there is no firm reason for the increase, there was no firm reason for the decrease. Maybe this hunger or desire for entertainment caused the increase and that same desire caused the dramatic decrease when new and better entertainment was found.

Regardless of the actual reason, by the time I joined Freemasonry in the mid-1970s there was true concern in the Grand Lodges about membership. Because the Grand Lodges were forced to expand their infrastructure to accommodate all the new members, the decrease in members, and reduced dues, were hitting the lodges and Grand Lodges hard. It was a money problem. Without the same level of membership that caused the expansions, lodges and Grand Lodges began to run into financial difficulties.

But then by the 1980s, another change took place. A book written by Michael Baigent, Richard Leigh and Henry Lincoln with the title *Holy Blood, Holy Grail* was published. It struck a resounding chord and became a bestseller. The book was basically a metaphysical mystery novel about the Knights Templar, Freemasonry, secret societies, and the Roman Catholic Church. It contained all the elements to grab hold of the interest of a society looking for something new. This was the book that ended up inspiring a whole series of books and movies by Dan Brown and others on the same subject.

All of a sudden, Freemasonry, along with an amazing mystery, was in the forefront of the public. It was truly the entertainment of the moment. Just like years earlier, Masonic membership went on the rise. You would think that this was a lucky break for Freemasonry. And for a little while it was a very good break. But it seemed that while many did join, they also left almost as fast as they joined. In many areas, it was a near revolving door of new members. Why?

Well, the answer to this question may be a little easier and clearer than the decrease in members in the 1960s and early 70s. Many of the young Masons who joined and quickly left were vocal about why they were leaving. Simply put, what they found in the Masonic lodge was nothing like the Freemasonry that they expected when they joined. Exactly what did they find and what did they expect? They expected enlightened mystics waiting to instruct them in the hidden miseries of the world. They found cantankerous old men eating green beans, reading minutes, and arguing over bills.

And that brings us to today and the divisions we now see in Freemasonry. On one side we have lodges that have existed for years pretty much on autopilot. Little to no education (and that would be Masonic education) has taken place in these lodges for longer than any can remember. They have become little more than second-rate social clubs consisting of a meal before the meeting and then the meeting consisting of reading minutes and discussing bills. Every now and then initiations take place. They are often done poorly and when they are completed, new members are introduced to Masonry not with education, but with the same routine of the business meeting.

Young Masons are often upset that their understanding of Freemasonry, the one that they held before they joined and saw in books and movies, doesn't seem to exist. Within the ritual and symbolism of Freemasonry, they can see where the teachings can and do exist. They maybe even once were worked and taught, but what happened? Why are we a shell of what we can be and maybe once were?

This is the division and the situation currently existing. One side wants more, and the other side believes that what we have now is Freemasonry. Both sides point to the other as the source of the problems. Who is right and who is wrong?

If we go back in time to the period just following World War II and the time of the unexplained dramatic increase in members, maybe we can find some answers.

When, suddenly, new members begin joining, changes were required in Masonry. It was necessary to accommodate all the new members. Grand lodges had to add new staff to properly account for the new members and do the necessary paperwork. But what about the Masonic work, the teaching and education of new Freemasons? Let's look at that.

When I joined Freemasonry in the mid-1970s, I was told by older members that there was a time when the lodge was filled with new members. By the time I joined the decrease in membership was already well underway. I had a knack for ritual, so I advanced rather quickly and right after my Master Mason degree I was placed in the office of Junior Deacon for a half year and then moved up to Senior Deacon that same year. The following year I was elected Junior Warden and went on to become Master two years later. I was told how many years earlier it took dedicated members quite a number of years to work their way through the chairs.

When I joined there were no active members serving as Stewards of the lodge. Technically there were Stewards on the list of officers, but they were not active — they didn't attend. They were just names placed on the officers' list to fill the holes needed. They were kept on the roster simply to give the appearance of a full officer lineup. But this was not always the case.

I was told of the time when not only was there a Senior and Junior Steward, but at least a half-dozen other Junior Stewards. The officers were required to attend all meetings and if any of the Junior Stewards missed a meeting or two without good cause, they were removed from the office. This rule was for all the officers. You were present and did the work or you did not advance. There were many others who were willing and eager to advance and do the work necessary. But right *there* was the problem of the large new membership. What was the work that was necessary and how was it accomplished?

Masonic educational classes had always been taught in the lodge by instructors who were skilled in Masonic ritual, symbolism, and philosophy. Instruction would take place by means of classes held on meeting nights, on evenings when there were no meetings, or on weekends. Instruction could also take place in the lodge, or at the home of the instructor.

The large increase of new members, however, placed a burden on the instructors. Where at one time they had one or two candidates for instruction, the large increase of new members made these classes of instruction larger. I believe that it's here that we can trace the lack of education and instruction. Simply put, the instructors were overwhelmed. There were too many candidates and new Masons for proper instruction. Instruction began to slide and become compromised.

The instructors were not experienced in dealing with large classes of instruction. It was a new situation and one that the instructors were not prepared to handle. Previously taught lessons were no longer being taught to the newer members. Candidates and new members, with only a fraction of the education previously given, began working their way into the chairs of the lodge. Education began slipping with a little being left out of each generation of new members.

In time, the semi-taught Masons became the instructors themselves. Semi-taught Masons soon became senior Past Masters and Grand Lodge Officers. These Masons, even if sincere and dedicated, could not teach what they were not taught.

And then came a dramatic *decrease* in members. Not only were lodges and Grand Lodges facing a situation where leadership was being filled by those with only *some* of the education necessary, but stations were being filled by whoever happened to be there, qualified, or not.

Not only was Masonic education slipping but also the dedication and quality necessary to hold office. The structure and integrity of the Masonic organization began to slip.

But for as long as I can remember, there has been an interesting situation that has existed in lodges. In looking back, I can think of the very early days in my Masonic career. There are some Masons who stand out in my memory. Some of these Masons had absolutely no interest in or knowledge of any part of the Masonic history or philosophy, and they were, frankly, horrible at ritual.

But these Masons were truly good and decent human beings. Whenever anything needed to be done, they were there. They were at every meeting and were always prepared to do whatever needed to be done at a moment's notice. If the lodge needed cleaning up, they were there. If a large purchase was to be made and a committee was needed to check out the various companies to see which was the best deal, they were there to serve on any committee. If someone's car broke down in the middle of nowhere in the middle of the night, one call to any of these brothers was all that was needed to bring help. They were not skilled in any of the Masonic history, philosophy, or ritual but they would give you the shirt off their back without hesitation. They would do whatever was in their ability to do for the lodge or any member.

These were the members who kept many of the lodges alive during the tough periods of very low membership. How can any thinking or reasonable Mason say that these Masons are not true brothers?

I believe that it's time that those on both sides of this division stopped for a minute and think. It is very true that Masonic education consists of the history, philosophy, and ritual of Freemasonry. It is also very true that many of the older members have little to no knowledge of many, if any, of these necessary Masonic skills. But I believe that it is just possible that the Masonic change that is taking place contains an aspect that we may not have thought about previously.

Humans are of a dual nature. We have a physical aspect and a spiritual aspect. Physically we live in this world and are affected by everything around us. We grow hungry, tired, affected by the climate and everything existing in the physical world. But we also have a spiritual side or a divine spark within us all. We have the ability to know right from wrong and the ability to feel sadness and joy.

Maybe, just maybe, this change that is taking place in Freemasonry is a natural one designed to match Freemasonry with the dual nature of humanity. Maybe it's important to have some lodges that are little more than social clubs composed of good, decent Masons with little to no desire for the deeper aspects of Freemasonry. Maybe it's also important to have other lodges that are centers of esoteric enlightenment.

Why is this a problem?

The only problem that I can see is when anyone tries to tell another the path that the other needs to take. We need to focus more on our own path, our own work, and allow the other guy the freedom and ability to follow whatever path he chooses. The change that may be required might deal with how we react to others and the respect that we should give to what they believe, want, and need.

I believe that the years of hard times have made some of us too possessive of our lodges. I've seen an almost fanatical attachment to lodges, even at times placing more importance on a lodge than Freemasonry itself. The idea of a lodge failing becomes an almost personal failure.

A new Mason who joins a lodge is sometimes taught that one must be loyal to his lodge regardless of what is offered or the condition or nature of the lodge. It is here that the validity of the arguments of some of the young Masons needs to be recognized. It is fine if one chooses to work in a lodge that is minimalistic in nature. I believe that a lodge that only reads minutes, pays bills, and acts as a social club *is* Masonic if that's what its members want, and it is not in danger of ceasing to exist. What is *not fine* is if someone joins that lodge, expects more out of Freemasonry, and then is told that he is disloyal if he leaves for a lodge more suited to his personal path.

We cannot be so possessive and selfish that we accuse our members of disloyalty or claim that they lack commitment if they do not find the working of our lodge acceptable to them. They are not automatically lacking in Masonry if they seek to find what they need in another lodge. All of us have the right to have the Masonic experience that we want and need. Once we recognize who and what we are, we can attract those of like mind and exist as a lodge as we choose. Of course, if the only way that we can exist is by forcing those who are not on the same path as us to remain with us under threat of insult or other pressure then we cannot, by any means, claim to be truly Masonic. True Masons do not adversely affect other Masons out of selfishness or try to force them into paths that they do not wish to follow. If the only way that a lodge can exist is by forcing members to remain members regardless of what they want and desire, then this lodge does not deserve to exist. Period.

All Masons deserve the right to follow whatever path they choose. On the other hand, if a lodge is successfully working on a minimalistic structure and this is the choice of the membership, then it also has the right to exist as it chooses. Masons should not try to force esoteric or deeper teachings on a lodge that does not understand or desire these teachings.

We should *all* find and work with, and in, the type of lodge that we choose. This is a right that should belong to everyone. It's okay to move to another lodge or other Masonic body more in line with our own views and thinking. It is not okay to force change that is undesired on anyone or to deny another sincere Mason from following his own path.

We must understand that sincere Masons and lodges can have differences of opinions and goals. We need to respect those differences and still be able to associate ourselves with lodges matching our own desires and views of Freemasonry. This is the only way that I can see us moving forward in a positive manner for the benefit of everyone.

Of course, none of this means that we should try to change reality. We can't call an apple an orange or Masonic entertainment programs, actual Masonic education programs. As long as we are real about who and what we are, we have the potential to exist in peace. We can grow.

Freemasonry is all about personal growth. Our long-professed claim is that we take good men and make them better. We do not claim to take good men and change how they think into how *we* think and what *we* want. Older and younger Masons need to recognize that the "other side" has the right to think and believe as they choose. We can't force what we want on others, nor should we allow what others believe or want to be forced on us.

Older Masons must recognize that the younger Masons can have a different path and that they are the future of Freemasonry. We must not step on them or attempt to change them. Younger Masons must recognize that the older Masons kept Freemasonry alive during very difficult times when they may have been in grammar school. In either case, nasty comments or actions are unfitting of any Freemason. Both sides need to look at the other with admiration for what they did in the past and what they can do in the future. We must come together, respect each other, and see the benefit of different ideas of Freemasonry.

My Brother's Keeper

Then the Lord said to Cain, "Where is your brother Abel?"
"I don't know," he replied. "Am I my brother's keeper?"
~ Genesis 4:9

When we say that we are our "brother's keeper," it is understood to mean that we are responsible for our brother. We watch out for our brothers and do what we can to keep them safe and on the right path. But why do we need to take care of someone else and is this something that we in fact do? In the Biblical story of Cain and Abel, Cain grew jealous of Abel. The jealousy grew into hatred and Cain eventually killed him. When God asked Cain about Abel, Cain's response was the equivalent of saying that he didn't feel that he was responsible for his brother and didn't keep tabs on him. His brother was not his problem.

The Bible teaches us many stories of how to live. It teaches us to be kind, generous, honest, and caring towards others. It teaches us to think less of the "me" and more of the "us." But also, from the beginning of time, man has struggled to live up to these teachings. Paradise was lost for a reason. Also, from the Bible we learn that brothers do not always support each other. Cain and Able are just one of the Biblical moral stories that teach of the dangers of greed, envy, or any of the lesser qualities of man. Too many times we look at someone else and find fault. We may believe that they are doing wrong yet gaining. *"Why is that guy getting this, this, and this and yet I work so hard and get so very little?"* We see only what we *believe* we know of "the other guy's" successes and failures. Envy, jealously, and ego take hold of us.

Masons call each other brother. We don't use the terms "friend" or "acquaintance." We say "brother." But why do we use this term? Do we say "brother" to show an intended close relationship that should exist between Masons? Did Cain have that close a relationship with Able? We say that we will not cheat, harm, nor allow anyone else to wrong our brothers. We claim to be our brother's keeper. We promise to be such. But, really, do we do that?

We live in a truly divided world. Time and again we see examples of the "me" being placed before the "we." We see anger, jealousy, unchecked ego, and we see a near total focus on one's own needs with little to no regard for anyone else. The "other guy" is only considered if he can play some role in helping "me." We, sadly, see this also in Masonry, maybe more often than we would like to admit.

So, why do we act so often only for "the me"? Why does it seem so very hard to be our brother's keeper? Do we harm ourselves when we help someone else? Is thinking of the other detrimental to our own best interests? Are we, frankly, stupid to not put ourselves first and help someone else only after we are certain that all our own needs are satisfied?

I can see, somewhat, how some believe that they will hurt themselves by helping others. Many claim that helping others could weaken them. It's the old concept of, *"If I give you some of what I have, I will have less and be weaker."* The "I" is far more important than the "we." But is that the best philosophy for society or any group? When I was a boy, I was wholly taken with *Aesop's Fables*. I would read them over and over. There is a fable from Aesop that I would like to offer that deals with this subject. It's called, "The Father and his Sons."

> *A father had a family of sons who were perpetually quarreling among themselves. When he failed to heal their disputes by his exhortations, he determined to give them a practical illustration of the evils of disunion; and for this purpose he one day told them to bring him a bundle of sticks. When they had done so, he placed the bundle of sticks into the hands of each of them in succession and ordered them to break it in pieces. They tried with all their strength and were not able to do it. He next opened the bundle of sticks, took the sticks separately, one by one, and again put them into his sons' hands, upon which they broke them easily. He then addressed them in these words: "My sons, if you are of one mind, and unite to assist each other, you will be as this bundle of sticks, uninjured by all the attempts of your enemies; but if you are divided among yourselves, you will be broken as easily as these sticks."*[1]

It is a falsehood that we are weakened by all working together. There is strength in numbers. There is strength in unity. It is not helpful to think only of ourselves. If we do not make sure that all of us are strong, then none of us will truly be strong. The concept of strength of numbers is as ancient as humanity and is valid.

The goal is for us to succeed, but the only way that we can do it is by acting as one. We are stronger when acting as one — as the bundle of sticks. So, why do some seek to divide us? Division weakens us. Maybe because blind ego plays a role. When we are one of many, we do not stand out for all the praise and rewards. To stand out, we must not be hidden by many others. Focus on the *me* can destroy the *us*.

In the craft lodge ritual of the Scottish Rite, the three "bad guys" are represented as Ignorance, Falsehood, and Ambition. It is Ambition that represents the final evil doer. Ambition uses Ignorance and Falsehood to take what he believes is his right, his reward for existence. It is an unhealthy logic that believes that one is due everything simply by their own existence. But it is a reality. There are those who will put their own wants and desires above everything else, above everyone else. In their mind, they are the only one to be considered as they are the only one who matters. These are the ones who will destroy everyone and everything around them (including themselves) because of their absolute belief that they are the only ones to be considered.

An unbridled ego requires the self to be viewed as the best, the one who is never wrong, the one who is always to be listened to and obeyed. Why? Because that is the way it is desired by ego. No other reason. If you do not understand or disagree, then you are the enemy. You must be crushed.

The three "bad guys" in the Hiramic Legend wanted a rank and all the power and glory that came with it. The fact that they had not earned it, and did not deserve it, did not matter. All that mattered was that they wanted it. That was it. They made it perfectly clear that they would kill a good man in order to get it. And they did kill him. They made good on their threat. But what did their action gain for them? Nothing. Not only did they not achieve what they wanted, they lived the balance of their lives in disgrace and on the run until the time of their gruesome deaths. Their attempt at power, glory, and titles brought them just the opposite. They destroyed everything around them simply for personal gain.

The Bible offers countless moral truths designed to help us improve who and what we are. In *Matthew 20*, we find a profound truth about leadership. It seems there was some discussion among the disciples as to which one was going to become the chief lieutenant of Jesus. Two of the disciples felt most qualified and were reconciling themselves to becoming the right and left hand of Jesus. When the other ten learned of the plans, they became upset. They felt that they should also be considered for these honored positions. They all worked hard and felt that their work entitled them to the rank and privilege of being leaders. When Jesus learned of the discussions and opinions, he told them that a misunderstanding must exist. He said that those who would carry on his work after he was gone would not be *leaders* but *servants*. Their job would be to assist others in learning and growing. They would not be in positions of honor, but service. That was quite different than the common thought of such positions.

If any of you have played team sports in school, then you know of the philosophy in sports of the team effort. Everyone works towards the goal of winning and they do so as a team. If one stumbles, the others help him and get him back on his feet. They win or lose as a team. Each has his own role, and they all work and support the team effort.

Freemasonry, as well as all of life, is a team effort. We are strengthened, not weakened by helping others. My struggles are your struggles, and yours are mine. We must be one to best survive in this world. We must grow and help each other grow. We are not here to force anything on anyone. But we must always be ready to put out our hand when needed. That's what it means to be our brother's keeper.

Notes:

1. Aesop, "The Father and his Sons," https://etc.usf.edu/lit2go/35/aesops-fables/388/the-father-and-his-sons/.

What Does it Mean to be Irregular?

Not long ago I received an email from a new Mason. He said that he met a Mason who identified himself as a 33rd degree Scottish Rite Mason. He then added that the Mason belonged to a jurisdiction not recognized by his jurisdiction. He wanted to know how he should treat him.

The Brother was serious, and it was clear that this situation had never been mentioned to him by any of the members of his lodge or his Scottish Rite Valley. He honestly did not know how to treat someone from an unrecognized jurisdiction. Let's look at this question.

First off, Grand Lodges maintain what's known as "Fraternal Relations" with other Masonic bodies, or they don't. This means that all the lodges under any jurisdiction that has Fraternal Relations with your Grand Lodge, are considered OK to visit. If Fraternal Relations *do not* exist, then visitation or discussion of things that should be reserved for a lodge at labor are usually not allowed. But it needs to be pointed out that each jurisdiction has its own rules. For more specific information as to the rules and regulations concerning visitation for you, I *strongly suggest* you contact your Grand Secretary's office.

But the problem that I sometimes see is Masons who get carried away with things. Some feel that if Fraternal Relations do not exist with another body, then it means that they have a right, or maybe even a duty, to be rude or unpleasant to the other person. In my opinion, this type of attitude is unMasonic and contrary to everything that we teach in Freemasonry.

We must obey the laws, rules, and regulations of our own jurisdiction, but at the same time we are not to be discourteous to others simply because they may belong to a jurisdiction that we don't today recognize. Lack of Fraternal Relations does not automatically mean irregularity. And even if someone is not a regular Mason, or not a Mason at all, it doesn't mean that they are not a good human being. A Mason is not a superior being simply by possessing regular Masonic membership. Our value as a human depends on our conduct and actions.

Let's look for a minute at Freemasonry in the United States. There are, for the most part, two types of recognized Freemasonry. That would be what's known as "mainstream" Masonry and Prince Hall Masonry.

Mainstream Masonry is normally the older Masonry and sometimes called the "white Grand Lodge." This is because there was a time in the history of US Freemasonry when if you were not white, you were not allowed to become a Mason. It was truly an unenlightened time.

Prince Hall Masonry was created to give African-Americans the same opportunity to join Freemasonry as those who happened to be born white. There was also a very interesting rule that became agreed upon in the very early days of Masonry in the United States. That rule was that there could only be one Grand Lodge per state. With that rule, any additional Grand Lodge became automatically irregular. You will find that in many cases, rules determine regularity rather than living the Masonic philosophy.

So, from its very early days in the late 1700s, Prince Hall Masonry was deemed to be irregular because it was technically an additional Grand Lodge, and it violated the rules. But, in reality, it was simply because its members were not white. Fraternal Relations did not exist between any Grand Lodge in the United States and its Prince Hall counterpart for nearly 200 years.

Over time, the idea that a Mason needed to be white was recognized as ignorant, hateful, and wholly unMasonic in most all jurisdictions. New Masons were made in "Mainstream" jurisdictions regardless of race. But Prince Hall Masonry was still considered outside of regular Freemasonry.

Everything changed in 1989 with the recognition of the Prince Hall Grand Lodge of Connecticut by the Grand Lodge of Connecticut. But there still existed that rule about only one Grand Lodge being allowed in a state. So, what did they do? A few Grand Lodges broke Fraternal Relations for a short time with the Grand Lodge of Connecticut. But they soon realized that this was not the right path. Their answer was to modify that troublesome rule.

The new understanding of the rule of Exclusive Territorial Jurisdiction became one Grand Lodge per state *unless* the Grand Lodge decides to enter into fraternal relations with another Grand Lodge in the same state. With that modification of the rule, we have today most US Grand lodges enjoying fraternal relations with their Prince Hall Masonic counterparts.

But think about exactly what it meant when a Grand Lodge recognized (entered into Fraternal Relations) with its Prince Hall counterpart.

Prior to a Grand Lodge and its Prince Hall counterpart entering into Fraternal Relations, did they view each other as regular? In many Grand Lodge proceedings, you'll find Prince Hall Masonry being defined as irregular. It was not until Fraternal Relations were established did they begin to call each other *regular*. Why? Did something change in the nature of either Grand Lodge that caused them to be viewed as regular? No. In all cases, the only thing that changed was that fraternal relations were established.

Freemasonry in the United States seemed to link the existence of Fraternal Relations with regularity and the lack of Fraternal Relations with irregularity. Once Fraternal Relations started happening between US Grand Lodges and their Prince Hall counterparts the definition of regularity changed.

But regularity must mean something apart from just the existence of Fraternal Relations. Regularity cannot be only automatically tied to, or understood as, the existence of Fraternal Relations. If we do so, then the recognition between US Grand lodges and their Prince Hall counterparts makes no sense at all.

Yes, there are established rules about regularity of origin, regularity of work and so on. But, so very much about regularity seems completely subjective.

Nothing about the nature of Prince Hall Masonry changed prior to or after its recognition. Prince Hall Masonry was, and is, regular Masonry that was just not recognized as such for many years — or it was never regular. This does not mean that every single organization that calls itself Masonic is regular by how we normally define *regular*. But it also does not mean that regularity is determined *only* by the existence of Fraternal Relations.

This brings us to another point.

I have seen some Masonic bodies that truthfully have no legitimate claim to regularity by how Freemasonry determines regularity. (And for *how* Freemasonry determines regularity, see your Grand Secretary's office for the particular details for your own jurisdiction.) However, some of the Masons who belong to some of these irregular bodies sure act like regular Freemasons.

How can we explain that?

Well, Freemasonry is all about an individual following a certain set of teachings in order to improve himself. These teachings are not secret. Our teachings are right there for the world to see.

So, if according to the rules of Freemasonry, some Grand Lodges are, after examination, determined to *not* be regular for some technical reason, does that mean that it's impossible for its members to benefit from the Masonic teachings? I don't believe that's true at all. Also, is it possible for *regular Masons* to benefit from the teachings of an *irregular Mason*? Think about that question for a while.

If you pick up any book or list of famous Masons, you will find Benjamin Franklin's name included. This highly respected scientist, journalist, inventor, statesman, and one of the Founding Fathers of the United States was also a devoted Freemason, and even Grand Master. In 1734, Franklin edited and published the first Masonic book in the American colonies, a reprint of James Anderson's *Constitutions of the Free-Masons*. What might not be usually understood is that the eyes of the United States Masonic community at that time, Benjamin Franklin was viewed as an irregular Master Mason. That's right. He belonged to a Grand Lodge that for technical reasons was not, at that time, recognized as regular.[1] And yet we claim him as a famous Freemason who is worthy of emulation — and he was!

And, what about this 33rd degree Mason that the young brother wrote to me about? Should we disregard all 33rds who belong to a body that may not be viewed, for some reason, as regular? Well, I should point out that John Mitchell died as an irregular Master Mason. Who was John Mitchell? Well, he was the first Sovereign Grand Commander of the Supreme Council Southern Jurisdiction, USA. That's the Mother Supreme Council of the World — the first Grand Commander of the first Scottish Rite Supreme Council. Yep, in the eyes of the U.S. Masonic community of that time, John Mitchell died as an irregular Master Mason.[2]

Of course, John Mitchell was not always viewed as an irregular Master Mason, but he became irregular because of technicalities regarding that old concept of only one recognized Grand Lodge per state.[3] So exactly what does *regularity* mean and how much stock can we place on it when we look at an individual Mason?

As I've mentioned before, Freemasonry is of a dual nature. We have both the Masonic philosophy and the Masonic organization. Each organization of Freemasonry, and that includes each Grand Lodge, has its own rules and regulations. The choice for the members is to obey the rules of their organization or not be a member. It's as simple as that.

When new Masons are not properly taught the rules and regulations of their jurisdictions, problems can and do develop. Visitation and who can and who cannot visit is often not properly taught to new Masons. This is why I advise over and over again that if anyone has questions about what is or is not proper in their jurisdiction *do not* go on-line and try to find out for yourself. You can ask a question and receive a completely correct answer for another jurisdiction that is completely wrong for your own jurisdiction. The best place to learn about your jurisdiction is your own Worshipful Master, educated members, your District Deputy Grand Master, or your Grand Secretary.

But again, we are talking about the organization of Freemasonry. The philosophy is different. Our philosophy is designed to help the individual improve himself. That's it. We also don't say how much, we don't say how little, and we don't say exactly how. We simply provide all Masons with teachings and symbolic instructions on how anyone who applies these teachings can live a better life.

The level of benefit from our teachings to the individual depends on the level of work they put into learning and living the lessons. These teachings are also not part of our secret instruction. The only common thing that's secret in Masonry are matters of recognition and initiation. All lessons to help improve our members are open and free to anyone.

So, if our goal is ultimately to make ourselves better, and we make the instruction of how to do this available to anyone, then we are in fact benefiting members of our organization as well as those who are not members but choose to take advantage of what we teach. This brings us to what may seem like very strange situations concerning the members of our organization. This is especially true if members of our organization *do not* take advantage of our teachings, and yet others who are not members do take advantage of what we offer.

So, who is the *real Mason*, a member of our organization who knows nothing about our teachings, or the nonmember or even the so-called irregular Mason who has taken the time to learn and benefit from what we teach? The members of our organization have dues cards. But there is no guarantee that they have benefited from, or even know much about, what we teach. The Master Mason or even the 33rd degree Mason may or may not know any more about the deeper Masonic philosophy than the average guy in the street.

On the other hand, one who belongs to an irregular lodge of Masons may truly walk in the philosophy of what we teach. This places us in an interesting position. What does it mean to be a Mason? Are we a Mason if we possess a dues card? Are we a Mason if we live and practice the teachings of Freemasonry?

All new candidates are asked where they were first prepared to be made a Mason. The answer is in the heart. When these individuals were first prepared to be made a Mason, they did not have a dues card. They were not members of our organization. I believe that in all things in life we must seek a balance and that sometimes (maybe more times than we realize) to grow we have to adjust how we think.

The organization of Freemasonry is limited to those who are members. The philosophy of Freemasonry is limited to those who take the time to study the Masonic teachings. There is no requirement for members of the organization to understand its philosophy. There is no prohibition for those who are not members of our organization to study and understand our philosophy. It is my opinion that those who are not members of our organization and yet take the time to study our philosophy and know our teachings are truly special human beings.

Those members of our organization who act superior to anyone else simply by virtue of their membership in our organization, or by any office they have held, or any degree that they have received display a particularly profound failure in the understanding of exactly what it is that we teach. Their Masonic foundation is built on the unsteady sand of ego.

Because of the rules, regulations, and laws of our organization we have limits on how we can interact with those who are not members of our own organization. But if we have any understanding of what we teach, then we must treat all Seekers of Light with the respect due those souls who understand and live by the Masonic Light.

We must acknowledge kindred spirits, maybe not through the limitations of organizational rules, but with the unlimited respect and admiration of those who truly walk the path that we should all walk. In other words, be nice, don't judge, respect kindred spirits, and act as a true Mason.

We are, and can be, so much more than just a dues card or a certificate with our name on it.

Notes:

1. *Proceedings of the Most Worshipful Grand Lodge of Ancient Free and Accepted Masons of the Commonwealth of Massachusetts for the Year 1914.* Poole Printing Company Boston 1915 pp 251-253.
2. Michael R. Poll, *The Scottish Rite Papers*, (New Orleans, LA: Cornerstone Book Publishers, 2020) pp 1-21.
3. Ibid.

What is Masonic Education?

I'd like to look at a situation that deals with a question that seems to be asked by leaders in more and more Masonic bodies. It's a question, however, that many answer very wrong. The question is: "What is Masonic education?"

Over about the last 10 or 15 years there has been a growing demand by many Masons for Masonic education. The empty business meeting where one could only hope to find a reading of the minutes and discussions of bills was becoming simply unacceptable for far too many. They joined Masonry to learn the many lessons professed to be taught by Freemasonry.

The dry business meeting offered nothing in the way of any assistance in gaining enlightenment. Those seeking more from the lodge experience were sometimes told by Masonic leaders to seek out that education in Masonic books. The logical question following these types of non-answers was, "*If I have to find Masonic education in books, that I can buy anywhere, then why do I need to pay money to this lodge?*" It's a fair question. While Masonic books can and do augment all Masonic education programs, nothing replaces an experienced instructor to explain what is provided in Masonic books.

Masons seeking more from the lodges in the way of education and receiving nothing began to walk. Grand Lodges started paying attention. After all, the Masons who left upset were not asking for something that was not promised to them. We do make the claim to make good men better. It is reasonable to say that an empty business meeting will not accomplish that goal.

And it was not only Grand Lodges that started listening to the cries for real education. The Scottish Rite, the York Rite and all bodies of Freemasonry felt the pressure for education. The problem for everyone was that education had been absent for so long in all the Masonic bodies that no one seemed completely certain as to the nature of Masonic education or what it really meant. For too many years Masonic bodies had operated as second-rate social clubs. Few were taught much of anything as to the actual nature of Masonic education or how to present a Masonic educational program.

The blame game of why this current situation exists doesn't matter. This is the state of Masonry that exists today. We need to deal with it or ignore it. If we ignore it, members walk.

In the attempt to deal with the issue, some lodges and bodies missed the mark and sometimes did not even realize that what they began offering was not *anything* close to what was being requested. Egos sometimes got in the way and then tempers would flare. Let's look at this situation.

A few years back, I wrote about being invited to a lodge that had a planned education event. The Worshipful Master told me that it was his goal to have educational programs at the lodge every month. He was excited and proud to show off his attempts at uplifting the lodge. I went to the lodge and eagerly awaited the presentation.

The brother stood up and gave a talk on how to do minor automobile repair yourself to save money. I didn't know what to say to the brother when he came up after the meeting looking at me for encouragement for his efforts. He honestly didn't realize that what he did was in no way Masonic education. But it is not just him.

I've seen and heard of many other events identified as "educational programs" that ended up being presentations on retirement plans, insurance plans, home repair, inexpensive vacations, personal safety, shopping tips, and on and on, even things like how soft drinks are bottled. Representatives from museums, zoos, hospitals, restaurant associations, the park service, and many more groups have made presentations. I've even seen politicians and popular entertainers speak about everything under the sun at lodges and bodies.

At some point we need to ask ourselves, how does any of this help us in understanding Masonic symbols or any of its many teachings? Simply put, it doesn't. It is just entertainment. It's not Masonic education.

It is not my intention to seem to be throwing rocks at leaders who are trying everything they can and know to build interest in their bodies. But please listen for a minute.

If we were a civic or social club, then any of these subjects would make outstanding presentations. But we are Freemasonry. Masonic education is the teaching of some element of Freemasonry. It is to help young and old Masons better understand any aspect of the history, philosophy, or workings of a Masonic lodge.

An educational program in a lodge should be on some subject that in some way provides answers or a better understanding of something taught or done in a craft lodge. A well delivered and detailed lecture on auto repair by a master mechanic might provide very useful information for everyone with a car, but it is not *Masonic* education.

If you are sitting in a Scottish Rite Valley meeting, then an educational program should be on some aspect of the Scottish Rite. If in a York Rite meeting, then education should be on the York Rite. So, on and so on for all the bodies.

Not long ago I received an email from a brother who told me that he was having difficulty in finding a suitable educational program for his Scottish Rite Valley. He told me that he had invited a speaker from the local electric company who gave a very interesting talk on the power grid. He said that he was growing frustrated as nothing that he seemed to do satisfied some of the valley members. He wondered if *anything* would satisfy them. He was actually trying to blame the members!

I tried to explain to him that Masons come to the Scottish Rite for a Scottish Rite experience. I pointed out that for some, you can stand up and tap dance and they will be satisfied. But others will only be satisfied with a Scottish Rite experience at a Scottish Rite meeting. I pointed out that a valley confers 29 degrees. All he would need to do is give a short explanation on one degree a meeting (if his valley meets once a month) and he would have almost two and a half years of educational programs all lined up and ready to go. And *all* of them would be on the Scottish Rite.

It is exactly the same with the craft lodge or the York Rite or any group or body of Masonry. There are countless available programs that match the body if we only think about what we are doing.

What is Masonic Education?

Masons need to understand who we are, what we are, what we do, and why we do it. They need to understand the basics of lodge operation as well as the often-obscure philosophy of our symbols. They may not ever be proficient in the ritual, but they need to understand what the degrees mean.

It is because education was for so long missing from our lodges that too many leaders today have no idea as to what they should offer in the way of Masonic education. Too many, unfortunately, become frustrated when their efforts are dismissed as unimportant, and their ego becomes offended.

In a baseball camp you learn baseball, not fishing. In a music class you learn music, not carpentry. Get where this is going? In a Masonic lodge, you learn about Freemasonry. It's not that hard and there are those willing to help.

Freemasonry During the COVID-19 *Pandemic*

This paper is being written on April 16, 2020. We are right in the middle of the COVID-19 Pandemic. History is being made and while it is (in my opinion) not at all the time to make judgments as to the actions taken by governments to protect their citizens, it is a good time to reflect on and record some of the activity that we see taking place. The world does seem to be a different place — and it may never be exactly the same again.

The last Masonic event that I physically attended was on March 16th & 17th, 2020. I was invited to give a lecture for the Grand Lodge of Mississippi. At that time, there was a lot of talk about the virus, but nothing was really shut down and no one seemed completely aware of how bad this situation was or would become. But precautions were taken. We didn't shake hands. We did "fist bump" greetings. We were made aware to be a bit careful. I could feel things were happening in the air. When we returned home, everything quickly shut down.

I am, for the most part, staying at home as directed. There is talk of opening some places before too long, but this is the way it is at the time of this writing. My wife and I go out only to get groceries (which we buy in larger amounts to allow us to stay in longer) or to the drug store to have prescriptions filled. Frankly, this whole new situation has hit my family rather hard. I don't mean physically hard; I mean emotionally hard. I know that testing for this virus was a bit late in happening and then mostly only available for those who are front-line workers. I've never been tested. As far as I know, I am fine. But because of reports that one could have the virus, but feel fine, how do I really know that I am "fine"? Out of a reasonable concern that I could be infected, showing no signs of it, but being able to infect others, I stay home and wear a mask if I need to go out. It's my part in trying to be of help to the community. The virus only spreads if we give it the opportunity to spread. Yes, it's a pain, and I don't like staying home, but I'm not 6 years old. This is about *us* and not just *me*.

I know some yell about their "freedoms" being denied by the states shutting everything down. I know that some feel so very put upon by being told that they could help spread a virus that they might not believe exists. I do know that the economy has been hit very, very hard. But it is time to pull together as one. If we remain fractured, then we all suffer — and, maybe, for much longer.

Every few days my wife and I take a walk around the block or a drive in the area — just to get beyond the four walls. We go to the grocery about 8 am, maybe once a week. We have found that this seems to be the best time in our area for encountering the fewest shoppers. There are generally two types of customers — those with masks and those without. My wife and I wear masks. Conflicting advice and opinions on wearing masks seems commonplace. Officials seem to advise it, and I'd rather err on the side of caution. I see no value in being a hardhead. It seems so little to ask.

We have also begun shopping online for groceries. We have never done this before, and I was not completely sure how it worked. But I was rather amazed at how easy it was to do. I simply selected what we wanted and put it in a shopping cart. That was it. It was like ordering anything from anywhere online. The prices were about the same as in the physical store and if we ordered over $35 or $40 (easy to do), then shipping was free. In a couple of days, the items were at the front door. Of course, it was not exactly the same, and we could not buy as if we were in an actual grocery. We limited our order to mostly things that were canned or in a box/bag. We didn't even try to order anything cold or any meats (I imagine it is possible, but we have not tried it yet). Because of the pandemic, there were also many items that were listed as "out of stock." We did what we could do.

Ordering online makes you preplan meals. Many times in the past we went to the grocery in the afternoon and bought what we wanted to eat that evening. It seems to be a new world, and I'm not sure it will ever fully return to the way it was before all this mess. Ordering online does not eliminate the need to go to the physical grocery, but it does mean that you can spend less time there.

Masonry has pretty much closed down in most all jurisdictions of which I am aware. Most did so because of state orders which were looked to for guidance. As to when lodge meetings will begin again, it's anyone's guess. In the meantime, I have seen quite a number of Zoom and other online venues for Masons to gather. I've attended a number of very good online educational meetings. I've even been invited to do online lectures and podcasts. Masons are finding a way to gather and share knowledge. This is very good.

But there is something else that I have been noticing. When I do venture out around the city lately, I have begun to see strangers waving at me as I pass by them. At first, I was confused and thought that it was someone I knew. But no, they were just saying hello to me, a stranger. That's different for a city! It is also different from what I see in some places on TV with angry crowds yelling at what seems to be anything that moves. I also see more couples and singles out taking walks, riding bikes, and ... smiling. What's going on? We're in a pandemic. Why do I see smiles? Why are they waving?

We are in very difficult times. There is no denying it. Many are dying, and even those who are not sick are suffering from a historic economic collapse. We are in a new situation, and no one, not even the "smart guys," can tell us with any certainty when things will be better or what we will face in the near or distant future. Yes, we still see harsh and stark divisions in us, but it seems that we are beginning to also see what is truly special about humans. In the middle of such hardships we, all of a sudden, start to see hands reaching out to help. We see the kindness and the desire to help others with less or in worse shape than us. We see the best of humanity. We may not see this in the headlines, but if you look you will find it. You see it in the streets.

I've seen lodges who are dark due to "stay at home" orders sending a few members out to bring groceries to the needy, the elderly, and the sick in their area. We are Masons and have the need to act like Masons. I've also seen people standing outside of hospitals (all following proper distancing) cheering for hospital workers at shift changes. I've seen these "cheering groups" outside of grocery stores cheering for the many once invisible heroes who do things like stock grocery shelves to make sure that we have food in the stores. Yes, there are always knuckleheads who only wish to yell about their own discomfort, but this is far overshadowed by the silent majority who go about what is needed for the good of us all. I know that we are far from being out of the woods, but I am proud, and I have great hope. Being a Mason now should not just be just a dues card holder in an organization, it should be a call to charitable duty. It truly is about *us* and not just *me*.

Forgotten Symbolism of the Festive Board

Recently, I was asked to give a talk about the Festive Board. I did some thinking about it and realized two things. I have never written or spoken about the Festive Board and when considering it, I can see the layers and layers of Masonic symbolism woven into the various ceremonies and even just the practice of the Festive Board. I'd like to look at just some of the symbolism.

At the very beginning, let me say that this will not be an instruction guide to holding a Festive Board. It is designed to look into its deeper aspects — aspects that may not always be apparent at first notice.

The first thing that I believe I should mention, is that there are different styles of events under the umbrella term of *Festive Board*. When we look at the Festive Board as it is practiced, we do not see just one formula or set of rules. Maybe this is because from the beginning of what we know of the Festive Boards and Speculative Freemasonry there were different styles. The English style and the French style of Festive Boards were as different as the cultures. While the core of the Festive Board is getting together and the sharing of something to eat or drink along with the exchange of ideas, the particulars of a Festive Board change from lodge to lodge or body to body. But there is one common aspect of all Festive Boards that I would like to look at for a moment. I would like to look at this concept of gathering in groups and the sharing of ideas.

The concept of humans gathering together over a meal or just around a campfire and sharing ideas goes back to the earliest days of mankind. We can go back to the days when humans lived as hunters and gatherers to see certain practices. Hunters would go out during the day and hunt whatever game they could find. They would bring their catch back to camp with them for the evening meal. Whatever they caught that day would be processed, cooked, and eaten by all in the camp. They would gather around the campfire, share the meal, and they would talk. Maybe they would talk about the events during the hunt, maybe they would talk of a new fishing spot discovered, or new ways to fashion sharp pieces of flint to their spear or arrows, or maybe they would just talk of life. But it was this talking and sharing of ideas, discoveries, and experiences that benefited the whole group. Humanity grew as a whole because of the shared experiences and ideas that were freely exchanged between humans.

In the days of the old Operative Freemasons, these builders would travel from village to village and town to town on construction jobs. This was how they made their living and fed their families. During the day, these Operative Masons would work on whatever building project they had accepted. At nightfall, they would end the day's work and have a meal. It was at this time that they would mingle with the people from the town or village. They did as early man had done. They spoke a bit about their events of the day and shared experiences or news from other places. Maybe they would talk about how a neighboring village discovered new ways to plant crops that proved successful. Maybe they would talk about news of bandits who attacked another village or anything having to do with the health, safety, or well-being of another village. The villagers benefited from the news brought to them as well as the construction of whatever the Masons built. The Masons benefitted by being able to bring valuable news learned in one village to another village. This increased their overall value to the villages and towns. It assured them of future work. They became more than just highly skilled builders. They became a source of valuable information in addition to their building skills. The villagers wanted them to come again to work and visit with them. They were valued guests.

The old Operatives developed, honed, and protected their reputations. A good reputation brought them more work. A bad one could mean much needed work going to another lodge. Don't forget that for the old Operatives, another lodge of Operatives were the competition. A good reputation was absolutely necessary for them securing future work. If they were able to secure work, they could feed themselves and their families. These lodges did not play around with anyone who might damage their reputation. If a worker showed up drunk and disorderly, that was it. He was out of a job, even if he was drunk after his construction work was over. The Masons were expected to always act respectably in public. If they didn't, the worker was not only out of work, but the lodge wardens usually made a great noise about kicking him out. *"Look at this unworthy worker! We believed him to be respectful and upright. He tricked us, and now we do what is necessary to keep our number worthy of working for you! The shameful one is gone and no longer associated with us!"* Exact words for someone being thrown out? Who knows? But, from the records we do have from the old Operatives, this was the message. They did not want or allow anyone to remain in their company who could damage their reputation.

As time moved on, Operative Freemasonry transitioned into Speculative Freemasonry and changes took place. The term *Freemasons* no longer applied only to those who earned their living in construction. The Speculative Freemasons did other things to earn a living, and their building was internal. They worked on building their character through symbolic moral lessons incorporated into the rituals and teachings. Actual tools used in construction became symbolic tools designed to teach life lessons. But the formal gathering together to share experiences and ideas was not done symbolically. It was an active part of Masonic life. Our personal goal may have been to build ourselves into better human beings, but we depended on others to help in our work. The Festive Board was a social, practical way of recreating the learning environment from the early days of man. Rituals and toasting practices were developed to provide the participants with an enjoyable time and encourage development through social interaction.

The elephant in the room was alcohol. Too much of it caused problems. In the Middle Ages, alcohol was the drink of choice. Soda was not invented and even tea (while becoming known) was not widely used in Europe in the 1700s. Water could be very unsafe. The result was that ale or mead was the drink of choice for the common man while wine was the drink of the upper class. All these drinks were purified for safety and alcoholic in nature. Care had to be taken in drinking anything. Too much made you drunk. Being drunk was unacceptable.

Festive Boards seemed to lean more towards wine with their meals and toasting. Maybe this was a desire to seem more in line with the upper class. But, regardless of which type of alcohol they drank, drinking too much of it resulted in problems for the Speculative Masons. The reputation of the self-profession moral organization could be damaged if its members became drunk and disorderly at their gatherings. Of course, we must appreciate that the damage Speculative Freemasons could personally suffer by one of their number guilty of public drunkenness was not as costly as with the Operatives. For Speculative Masons, such displays by one of their number could, maybe, cause a decrease in membership.

For the Operative, it could mean the difference between the worker eating or not. Speculative Masonry did not suffer the same level of damage with publicly unruly members as did the Operatives.

While Speculative Freemasonry did not suffer the same actual loss from public drunkenness as did the Operative Masons, there still was a concern. Speculative Freemasonry took its role in society seriously. The teachings provided by the lodge were designed to "make someone better." Public drunkenness does not represent being made "better." Written into the laws of Freemasonry was a clearly defined moral code of conduct for its members. Those who violated any aspect of this code could and would be subject to Masonic trial. Public drunkenness has resulted in more than a few Masonic trials. But, in the early 1900s there came an even greater reason to prevent public drunkenness.

A movement began in the late 1800s to curb the use or abuse of alcohol. Several religious groups in the US felt that alcohol was a main cause of social deterioration. But it was not until December 1917 that the United States Congress passed the 18th amendment. It took until 1920 for this amendment to be ratified and put into use. The Eighteenth Amendment prohibited *"the manufacture, sale, or transportation of intoxicating liquors"* but not the consumption, private possession, or production for one's own use. Basically, it meant that if you wanted to make beer, wine, or any other type of alcohol in the bathtub and drink it yourself that was fine, but you could not buy it in stores. This prohibition on the sale or transportation of alcohol lasted until December 1933 when the 18th amendment was repealed by the 21st amendment.

During the ten to fifteen year period when the sale of alcohol was outlawed, there was no common use of alcohol in

Masonic lodges. It was no longer a social choice; it was against the law. By the time the 18th amendment was repealed, a social stigma had developed concerning the use of alcohol. This stigma remained, especially in what's known as the Bible Belt area of the United States. Festive Boards, long identified with serving alcohol, fell out of favor and were rarely held. Then Grand Lodges in the US placed prohibitions on the use of alcohol into their constitutions. Even after the 18th amendment was repealed these rules against the use of alcohol in Masonic lodges remained. Public drunkenness, while never actually tolerated by most lodges, became more of a valid reason for Masonic trials to be held.

I joined Freemasonry in the mid-1970s in Louisiana. At that time, alcohol was outlawed by every Grand Lodge of which I was aware. Festive Boards were simply not allowed as they were assumed to require alcohol. I remember reading about and asking about Festive Boards in my early days of Masonry. I was simply told that they were not allowed. Alcohol was given as the reason for these events being prohibited. The suggestion seemed to be that if alcohol were placed anywhere near Masons, they would drink enough to become drunk and disorderly and then trials would have to be held. I found the assumed lack of control in Freemasons by the Grand Lodges disturbing. Why would Grand Lodges assume that a glass of wine (which anyone could drink at home) would cause Freemasons to throw all the Masonic teachings out of the window? Did the Grand Lodges know something about Freemasons that I didn't know?

I soon found out that there was no current logical reason for the prohibition of alcohol in lodges. It was just the way it was done. It was one of those *"it's always been done that way"* kind of things. By the time that I joined, and in the years following, Grand Lodges were very concerned and focused on declining memberships. Lower membership translated into less income which meant trouble paying for things. That seemed to be far more of a real problem than if Masons could have a glass of wine or a beer in their lodge. It seemed unimportant if lodges could have Festive Boards. The matter was rarely, if ever, brought up in my early days of Masonry.

The Festive Board became an ignored relic of the past. At times, I also heard it spoken of in very disapproving tones simply because of the presence of alcohol in its ceremonies. The presence of alcohol seemed to be a symbol of an "unworthy" past relating to the practices of Freemasonry. But, after some time, a change took place. Alcohol seemed to no longer be the issue. To mention a Festive Board to some in Grand Lodge would result in stern lectures on the dangers of a Festive Board. It was then said to be *wholly improper*, but the subject of alcohol was minimized as it was claimed to never be the "real" issue. So, what was the issue with a Festive Board if not the alcohol?

Soon things became clear. For so very long we had been without the deeper lessons of the philosophy of Freemasonry. Few in the leadership knew much about them. This could be understood to mean that there was either a lacking in the leadership or that these teachings were not actually that important. Guess which answer was accepted?

The Festive Board was viewed to be undesirable as *something* in it was problematic for the leadership in days gone by. It would take time to dig up the problem, but past leadership did find it unfit for a lodge. Alcohol was used in the festivals, but that must have been a separate issue. The bottom line was that few knew the reason behind a Festive Board, and they did not know why alcohol was used. They didn't have any tangible answer and did not feel compelled to find an answer. Other problems seemed more important and deserving of their attention. The subject of the Festive Board and reviving them was just not considered worthy enough to waste spending too much time.

Ironically, following my study of the Festive Boards, a few forgotten aspects of the Festive Board became clear. The drinking of alcohol was not of great importance in the deeper meanings of the Festive Boards. In the early days of these Boards, it was important to keep from getting sick from bad water, but not today. It was the act of toasting that was important in these ceremonies, not what they drank. Toasting can be achieved with any beverage.

What I found to be a fascinating aspect of the study into Festive Boards was that by the late 20th century it seems most in leadership had forgotten, or never learned, much about Festive Boards. They seemed to know the term, but they didn't seem to understand much else about them. What was also interesting, was that during the time of Probation, when alcohol was removed from the lodges, it seemed that they did not realize that alcohol could be substituted with other beverages for toasting. It seems that it was felt that toasting with alcohol was the heart of a Festive Board. When they removed alcohol from the lodges, they felt that this killed the Festive Boards.

The irony was that the actual heart of the Festive Boards was the gathering together to share a meal and the discussing of ideas. The toasting and other ceremonies were simply add-ons that were felt to augment the whole event. Neither Prohibition nor later times stopped Masons from gathering to share meals before or after lodges. These events have always existed and have always been an important part of the total Masonic experience. It is just that we stopped calling these meals "Festive Boards" when the toasting and alcohol went away. It stopped being an event with ceremonies and then just continued as a gathering for meals, visiting, and discussions.

Ignorance of the history, philosophy, and nature of Freemasonry has plagued us for too many years. Yes, due to declining numbers, and the decreasing standards (too many years of near non-existent Masonic education) Masons who would not have been considered for leadership in the past have been elected to such positions. This has happened and it is happening. Of course, we can do nothing about the past. Some have sincerely tried to do all in their power to help, others have enjoyed allowing their egos to run in the park. It's time for everyone to get real and work together.

Masonry is not a collection of mumbo-jumbo rituals that are unknown because we "no longer work in nonsense." It is a profound system of moral education. By applying its teachings, we *can* be more productive and useful human beings. The Festive Board is a beautiful and long employed practice for all of humanity, not just Freemasonry. Yes, Freemasonry has borrowed this very old practice and created beautiful and meaningful ceremonies around it. I've recently attended a Festive Board with individuals at the same ceremony toasting with wine, others with iced tea, and still others with water. It was beautiful and meaningful regardless of the drink.

We must again start taking advantage of our forgotten ceremonies and rituals. In them we can find far more beauty than we may realize. So very much is right at our fingertips waiting to be discovered.

Is Freemasonry a Moral Philosophy?

It's not uncommon for brand new as well as long-time Masons to ask questions about aspects of Freemasonry. So much of how we do things, why we do things and the meanings behind our symbols are, for the most part, unknown to many of our members. The simple truth is that many of us did not receive the Masonic education that we should have received during and following our three degrees. Questions about the nature of Freemasonry are almost routine. Who are we? What are we? We often claim to be one thing but act like something else.

Whatever we know or don't know, there is something that we should keep in mind. No matter what anyone believes or thinks, Freemasonry is *not* a club. It's not a social club. It's not a civic club, and it is not a charitable club — even if we sometimes act like one. Of course, a Masonic lodge may act like a club (and that's fine if that's what its members want), but Freemasonry itself is certainly not a club. Freemasonry, as defined in our ritual and teachings, is a profound system of moral philosophy designed to provide enlightenment to our initiates. We make available to them, through instruction by symbols, the tools to improve their lives and become better citizens. But... are we so sure that this is our actual nature and what we do? What is a moral philosophy? How does anything written in old books apply to today's Freemasonry?

Moral philosophy is generally understood as one of the components of philosophy dealing with ethical questions of living and interacting with others. With it, we can explore human relations and learn how to coexist in an often difficult and problematic world. Moral philosophy is said to have three general branches. One branch deals with big picture issues such as "What is truth?" or "What is justice?" Another helps us in understanding concepts such as right and wrong. Then a third branch deals with practical concerns or dilemmas such as criminal justice, war, or even minor moral questions such as should someone lie to help another out.

In our Masonic degrees and rituals, we are presented with moral lessons and guidance designed to assist us in living more successfully within society. We are taught the importance of helping others, loyalty to our country, and how we should interact with our family and neighbors. We are taught not to cheat or be violent with each other. We are also taught to warn another if we see them about to stray from the path. Above all, we are taught of the Almighty's guiding Hand in all of creation. Clearly shown is the importance of the teachings within the Bible and how each Mason's Holy Book should be used, studied, and put into practice. We are taught to be good and just.

The many moral lessons that are within Freemasonry do, indeed, constitute a moral philosophy. Look for a minute at the Hiramic Legend. The Grand Master in this story could have compromised his honor and integrity by giving others what he promised not to give. After all, they were threatening him! But he knew that while he had no control over their actions, he had total control over his. They were not talking about his being passed over for a title or honor if he refused them. They were talking about taking his life. They wanted something from him, and if they did not get it, they promised to *kill* him. Fully understanding that they would make good on their threat, he firmly rebuffed them. Yes, he did pay the ultimate price. But, what about the price that *they* paid? We have little choice in how we will inevitably die, but we have complete choice if we live with integrity or not. That cannot be taken from us. That is solely ours to keep or lose. Nothing would ever change that he kept his integrity and that they lost theirs. The Hiramic Legend is clearly a profound lesson in moral philosophy.

Our problem in Freemasonry is not that we have no moral lessons. It is that we present them during degrees and then quickly move on to other things. It is like having a glass of fine wine and gulping it down in one large mouthful. We have a moral philosophy, but it can become lost or ignored in a flood of other unexplained aspects of our degrees. We can skip right by the meaning of our symbols without really understanding their importance. We move on to the other activities of the lodge. We can become influenced by ego or shiny trinkets of power. We very well may gain many titles and offices but never fully grasp Freemasonry or its nature.

So, what is there to do? I believe that we should live Freemasonry. We should contemplate our moral teachings. We should recognize that integrity is more than a word and that Freemasonry is far more than a club. We should become what our teachings say we should be by putting them into practice. It's probably a hard thing to do, but just as anything of true value, it is worth the effort.

Is it OK to Laugh?

A while back I was contacted by someone who made an interesting claim. He said that he wanted to talk with me about something that I had said, "some time back." He asserted that I said, "laughter has no place in Freemasonry" and he wanted me to expand on that comment. I had no idea what he was talking about. I told him that I had never made such a statement. Maybe something I said was misunderstood, but I never said anything about laughter having no place at all in Freemasonry. I believe that if laughter did not belong in Freemasonry, then Freemasonry would have no place for me.

But I also believe very firmly in balance. There is a time and a place for laughter and fun. For example, it is very inappropriate for laughter or kidding around to take place during a degree or any aspect of ritual. But that hardly means that there is no place in Masonry for good humor or lighthearted activities. We just must understand enough about Masonry to know when laughter is appropriate and when it is not. It truly is all about balance. The concept of balance plays a large part in a successful Masonic experience. And it doesn't matter if we are talking about a craft lodge, a Scottish Rite body, a York Rite body, or any organization in Masonry. If we go too far in any one direction, we fall out of balance and we will, before too long, find ourselves in trouble. Let me try to explain.

Problems come in Freemasonry when we display bad judgment by maybe taking a good thing a little too far. There is a difference between laughing with someone and laughing at them. If anyone in a lodge feels that they are the subject of ridicule, then they will not share in the enjoyment of the laughter. If during a degree the candidate feels that he has been made fun of, then the entire degree is a waste. The members will have taken the most important lodge activity and insulted the candidate, the lodge, and all of Freemasonry.

We must know when it is time to laugh and when it is time to be serious. We must know limits and when things have been taken too far. If we don't know, then we must learn or recognize that we are part of the problem in Freemasonry. If we turn a Masonic experience into a silly experience, then we have taken things too far. It is not unlike pornography. We may not know how to exactly put into words when something turns into pornography, but when we see pornography, we know it.

The lodge experience was never intended to be a joyless, unemotional, or dry experience. If the Worshipful Master knows how to laugh and knows where and when it is appropriate to laugh, then the lodge experience can take on new levels of enjoyment. I very much believe in the old saying, laughter is the best medicine. If we have good judgment, balance, and the ability to know what constitutes going too far, then laughter in a lodge can be a very important part of a successful lodge experience.

Forbidden Subjects in Lodge

As we know, Freemasonry is a system of laws, rules, and regulations. Some are obvious, but some might need a closer examination. I'd like to consider the prohibition of discussing religion or politics in a lodge at labor.

From the very earliest lessons in Masonry, we are taught that there is something greater than us — a Creator, a Grand Architect of the Universe. We also use the Bible in our degrees, and it is open in every lodge at labor. But we are very careful not to tell any candidate or member as to the particular religious faith they should join or belong.

Aside from assuring that a candidate has a sincere belief in a Supreme Being, Freemasonry does not interfere in a member's religious faith. Freemasonry most certainly does not elevate any one religion over another. In fact, discussions of the qualities of the various religious faiths have historically been prohibited in Masonic lodges.

The reason we don't discuss religious faiths in lodge should be clear — we do not wish to even give the appearance of favoring one faith over another nor seem to be making light of anyone's religious faith. Each member must decide matters of religion for himself and not have to deal with interference from members of the lodge.

The same is true of politics. Freemasons must obey the laws of their city, state and country as well as be peaceable citizens. But opinions concerning how the government should best operate and which political party is "the best" is left up to each Mason to decide for himself. Freemasonry is no more a political party then it is a religion.

Individual Freemasons may have strong support for a particular political party, or some political candidate, but that should not be understood as Freemasonry *itself* having any position at all regarding politics or politicians. It would be perfectly acceptable for a Worshipful Master, or any member, to announce that important elections are coming up. It would also be perfectly acceptable to advise all members to go out and vote. It would *not* be acceptable, however, if any member told other members in lodge *how* they should vote in some civic election.

But recently, I've had very interesting discussions with Masons about situations that have developed in a few lodges. I've been told of lodges where all the attending members held the very same political or religious opinion. In such a case, the question was asked if it would then be acceptable for pointed discussions of religious or political ideology to be held in these lodges. After all, since they all agreed, there would not be any arguments, nor would the peace and harmony of the lodge be broken. Well, no, I don't believe it is proper to have such pointed discussions in a Masonic lodge regardless of the professed opinions of the members.

Let me explain.

I may very well believe something strongly today, but I can change my mind tomorrow. That is my right. I can change my mind on anything at any time. The reason we do not allow such discussions of religion or politics in a lodge at labor is because the lodge is to be a place of peace and harmony. Many can be very passionate about their religion or their political opinions. These are subjects that can cause disharmony and outright arguments in lodge or anywhere. Just because all the members present in the lodge agree on something today, does not at all mean that they will agree tomorrow.

And, what about members of a lodge that do not attend regularly or visitors coming into the lodge? Prohibitions are placed on these subjects because discussions of these subjects can break the peace that should exist in a lodge. Just because everyone believes *this* today does not mean that half will not believe *that* tomorrow. It makes sense to keep discussions of religion and politics out of the lodge.

Having said the above, I do not mean, at all, that discussions of Masonic symbols or teachings that appear in the Bible should be avoided. The Bible is on our Altars because it is from here that Freemasonry draws many of its lessons and teachings. In many lodges you will see the Book of Faith of a number of different religions. Freemasonry is, and always has been, a *religious* organization. There is nothing at all wrong with giving a symbolic teaching from any religious faith. As long as everyone realizes that we are not advancing one faith over another, then we are on safe ground. Freemasonry respects and honors all religious faiths and will not dictate the faith of its members.

But there is something else that I've seen at various times that has gotten more than a few lodges in hot water. It is when lodges that have websites or social media pages publicly endorse or run political ads for various candidates on their lodge website or social media pages. Lodges should not become involved in this sort of activity for obvious reasons.

Yes, lodges should support their country. Yes, lodges should display the flag and encourage everyone to vote and exercise their rights. What lodges do not want to do is become any sort of tool that can cause political or religious division within Freemasonry. It is one thing to announce that Bro. John Smith is running for a political office. That is news. It is another thing to tell all the members on the lodge website to go out and vote for Bro. Smith.

Freemasonry is not a religion, nor a political party and we do not advance one opinion above others. We are very free to speak our minds on anything at all if we do not represent that we speak for Freemasonry or express these opinions in lodge. We are not to spark disharmony in the lodge. We must respect the right of every Freemason to have and hold his own opinions on matters of politics and religion. Freemasonry itself cannot take sides in such personally important and private decisions.

Our religious and political opinions should be held and arrived at after considerable, serious thought. We should afford others the same rights and privileges. One's religious faith, as well as his political opinions, are private and need not be debated with others to be acceptable. We don't have to prove that our religious belief or political opinion is valid to others. We should all arrive at our beliefs after serious thoughts and personal considerations.

We should respect our own faith and opinions as well as the faith and opinions of others. After all, to be respected we need to give respect. Our religious faith and political opinions need to be acceptable only to us. It is very wise to keep discussions of religion and politics completely out of the lodge. Our lodge halls are a place to grow in Light, not argue as to who holds "the correct" belief.

How (and will) You be Remembered?

There is a time for us all. No matter if we are rich, poor, good, or bad; a day will come when we have no further use for this physical body. We can't do anything to change that fact. We also can't change that too many will believe *anything* about others, even if it is nonsense. Many things are beyond our ability to control. But there are things that we can control.

While we have no control over what others think, believe, or say, we have total control over our own thoughts and actions. We have the ability to travel our own chosen path and to even change paths in mid-stream. We can crumble if others think unfavorably of us, or we can recognize that others have the same rights and choices of belief as us. If others want to believe the worst of us, we can toughen ourselves. We can go on with our work and make our only thought the work that we are doing. We must believe in ourselves and what we are doing, or we will fold up and shut down. What another chooses to think or believe is more often than not a reflection of their own limitations. We should wish them well and go on with our work.

So, does this mean that we should not be concerned about our legacy, and what others will think of us after we are no longer physical? I don't believe it does. It means that we should always strive to improve and do the best that we can at all times. But doing our best doesn't mean that we should expect perfection. We are, after all, human and subject to all human frailties and imperfections. We should seek the balance between understanding that mistakes will happen and the effort to avoid as many slips as possible.

Albert Pike wrote: *"What we have done for ourselves alone dies with us; what we have done for others and the world remains and is immortal."* That is an inspirational line, but it is also a warning. What we do for others will be remembered and become immortal, but *how* it will be remembered depends on its help or hindrance to others. After all, Hitler *is* remembered. But how is he remembered? All actions have consequences. If we do good, then good will be remembered of us. If we do harm, either by knowingly doing so or failing to make the right calls, then that is what will be remembered. We must always balance what we do with what we deep down know that we should be doing.

We are, sadly, in a time when someone who truly means well can still do great harm. Our lodges advance far too many lacking the necessary Masonic skills and ability for their office. They are, at best, mediocre. They can make serious errors and fail to even recognize that a disaster took place. It's not really their fault as many of them were asked to take this or that position. (Remember, the ones asking you to accept something may not always be doing you a favor!) But great damage can still be done by one with the very best of intentions. Ego and *"it's the way it has always been done"* get in the way far too often. The legacy such individuals leave (if they even think about such things) may not be as they expect. Years after they are gone, the one with good intentions may be held accountable for a string of irresponsible acts. He may even be blamed for the death or down-turn of Masonic bodies. The unfavorable legacy may be all from well-meaning decisions that were not completely considered nor made in the sole best interest of Freemasonry. The disgraced leader may be memorialized as a serious drawback to, and failure in, Masonry. Who wants to be remembered like that?? History is neither on anyone's side nor against anyone. It does not concern itself with feelings. It is just the reflection of what is known, even if faulty or incomplete.

What we do or don't do has consequences. If we are in any position of leadership, then our actions will one day be judged, and we will have no say at all in the verdict. Our job right now should be to, with a clear mind, evaluate every possible action and outcome. If all we do is gather up titles and honors, then one day they may all be ignored under the blanket of disgrace. It is not enough to do what is good or right (by however we define those words). We need to do what is Masonic. And the only way to act and do what is Masonic is to make *very sure* that we properly understand the teachings of Freemasonry. If we don't know, *learn!* By doing this, not only do we have a far better chance of securing a positive legacy, but the ones we lead will get true Masonic leadership. Win-win.

The Reality of Masonic Education

I receive emails and messages from Masons on a regular basis asking questions about various aspects of Freemasonry. Many questions I can answer without much trouble, some require a bit of research, and some I can't answer at all. Also, every now and then I receive e-mails from anti-Masons or conspiracy theorists telling me that Masons control the world and so on. I tend to ignore these emails. But, about a week or so ago, I received an email that didn't fit any of these categories. It had to do with Masonic education in general but more specifically with me. The Brother had some nice things to say about what I was doing in Masonic education, said it was very needed, but was critical of how he believed that I was doing it.

I'd like to talk a little about what this brother said in his email and apply it to Masonic education. The brother told me that he has been a Mason about ten years. He said that his lodge has been in trouble most of that time. Lack of education and interest in most anything the lodge did plague his lodge, and many were almost ready to throw in the towel. He said that someone directed him to the videos on the New Orleans Scottish Rite College. He said that the videos there are exactly what is needed by his lodge, and he began showing them to the members. Because the videos are not "highbrow" or "over the heads" of the members, he said that his lodge benefited from the content. That pleased me and made me feel that all the work was worthwhile. But then, he threw in something that confused me.

He wanted to know why I was trying to keep the video channel, and Cornerstone Book Publishers a "secret." He said that he has been an active Mason since he joined and has never heard of me, or the videos, books, or podcasts. He said that if I am not willing to share what I offer, then why do I do it? He then said that Masons need what I am producing and that I should not keep it within a small circle. That hit me hard and aggravated me to no end. I took a few days to think and consider everything.

I'd like to give some information on the reason I started on this particular path and some of the obstacles faced. I'd also like to look at a few of the goals that lodges and individual Masons should set if they are serious about Masonic education.

My start in Masonic book publishing came as a result of my becoming aware of lists of recommended Masonic books in my early days of Masonry. These were book lists published by Grand Lodges and several Masonic research groups that recommended various Masonic books for Masons. I would become annoyed when I read these lists of suggested books only to find out that many of them were long out of print and, mostly, unavailable. I couldn't understand how we were supposed to learn about Masonry if we received sparse education in lodge and the Masonic books that could help us were mostly inaccessible.

So, in the mid-1990s I began reprinting old Masonic books that I felt were of value. I focused on quality books in various areas of needed Masonic education. I've published old reprints, Masonic philosophy, history, symbolism, books for the new Mason, the lodge officer, general interest, and books that other authors and I have written.

As Kindle began growing as a medium, I published as many as possible on Kindle. I've done audio books, Masonic podcasts, and for the past 7 years, Masonic and Scottish Rite educational and informational videos. I utilize websites, social media, and anything/everything available to let those with an interest know of the books, videos, and podcasts.

All anyone with any interest in my work needs to do is search my name, Cornerstone Book Publishers, or the New Orleans Scottish Rite College in Google or any search engine. You will find a list of places to go for the material or information you seek. I'm not, by any stretch of the imagination, trying to keep the work a "secret."

At the same time, I am a small company. Yes, every book that I have published is listed on Amazon and most of the on-line booksellers. But they may not always be easy to find. You may need to do a bit of searching for them on these bookselling sites. This is true of Cornerstone as well as other Masonic publishers.

Of course, there is not a great deal of personal monetary profit from the publishing of Masonic books. So, none of the publishers have huge advertising budgets. We do all that is possible. But truthfully, Masonic education is something that should be within the responsibility of lodges.

I know that because of a host of problems, not the least of which is new or inexperienced members being shoved into leadership positions long before they are ready, too many lodges simply do not realize that with just a little effort, very good educational material and programs can be obtained and presented to their lodges. Over time, entire Masonic education plans became forgotten or wholly unknown. There are things that your lodge can do to help.

Most lodges have email or printed newsletters (if your lodge doesn't, you should start one). The lodges send out these newsletters on a regular basis, usually once a month. Many lodges use these newsletters themselves as sources of Masonic education. If your lodge does not have a newsletter, contact the Secretary or Master of any neighboring lodges to ask for samples of their newsletters. Or go on social media and ask. You can get many easy ideas for interesting and useful newsletters without a great deal of effort.

Many times, a lodge secretary or Master handles the writing and publishing of the lodge's newsletter. But really, most of the time they have enough to do already. It is often wise to appoint someone other than either of these officers to oversee the newsletter. By sharing the responsibilities, you not only make each job less stressful, but it will make the newsletter usually more of an interesting and useful lodge tool.

Without a great deal of work, whoever edits a lodge's newsletter can find the names, addresses and websites of Masonic book publishers and booksellers. Just Google, "Masonic book publishers," or "Masonic book sellers," or just "Masonic books." List these names and addresses in your newsletter so that your members can have easy access to Masonic educational material.

Also, without much effort, you can find on the internet a great number of Masonic on-line educational programs. These may be YouTube programs, podcasts, or any number of on-line Masonic education sources. List these names and web addresses in your newsletter as well as book sources. Just these two things alone will increase the Masonic education potential of your members.

But what you can do to help your lodge and its members does not stop with these lists. Without question, Masonic books provide valuable information for Masons. But they also generate questions that may not be answered in the books. Masonic book clubs are proving very useful and enjoyable in many lodges. How they work is simple. Masons in a lodge (or an area) select a particular book to study. They all buy that book. Then they gather at regular intervals to discuss the book, ask questions, and share what they understood and took away from the book. This makes each book more valuable as questions about something in the any book may be answered in such gatherings. Since most Masonic book publishers provide generous discounts on bulk orders, by planning these book club events in advance the members can save money and have good educational experiences.

Another way to help your lodge as well as throw business to publishers is to invest in a lodge library. By selecting books that cover as wide a range as possible, you can build up a good Masonic library, and if you make the purchase all at once, the lodge can likely save a good deal with discounts from the publishers. Some lodges use their libraries as an active part of the lodges plan for Masonic education by allowing members to check out books to read at home. Masonic encyclopedias are a basic part of any lodge library, and no lodge should be with one or more.

I have seen Masonic presentations in lodges where members promote Masonic lapel pins, coins, mugs, aprons and even polo shirts or other clothing for the lodge to buy. But I don't ever recall being present in a lodge when they held up a Masonic encyclopedia to buy for the lodge or any collection of books that could be added to their lodge library — if they have one.

Yes, I get orders from a few lodges, Grand Lodges and Scottish Rite valleys for books, but they are few and far between. Many, frankly, act like they are only doing me a favor by buying the books. Some even have told me that my promoting Masonic books is looked at as if I am trying to just use Masonry to make money. Really?

See the Catch-22 situation? If I try to promote the books, some criticize me for "trying to make money off Freemasonry." If I just do the work and say little, then I am criticized by others for not letting them know what is available. If I give up and walk away, then I am criticized again for giving up. And the fact that my "profession" makes me, at best, little more than working in fast food restaurant, does not help. All the while the promotion in lodges for the flashy looking coins, mugs and clothing goes on while we profess our desire for Masonic education. Not much education is going to come from a coin or mug.

I've written often on what lodges can do … or don't have to do. Really, a lodge can operate however it likes. No education has to take place. And yet, some lodges can have serious education. Or, they can have a mixture. But, if we say that we want education, then we must do what is needed to obtain it. What we can't do, without harm, is to profess one thing, but do something else.

No lodge should be without a Bible, a handbook of law or a monitor from their jurisdiction. But, if a lodge says that it wants education for its members, then it should, at the *very* least, have a Masonic encyclopedia for their member's use. You don't have to buy your books from Cornerstone. You can go on-line or to a used bookstore in your area. But you need good Masonic books for your lodge. It's as simple as that.

If your lodge has decided that it wants to move in the direction of education, then it needs to have a library of Masonic books for the members to review and learn from. In addition to one or more encyclopedias, it needs books on Masonic history, philosophy, and symbolism. How large a library you end up having is up to your lodge.

If you say you want to be an educational lodge, but only budget for pins, coins, and mugs, then you are kidding yourself. You need to have Masonic books in your lodge, and you need to *tell* the members which books they should buy for their own personal study. We can't expect new members, or any members, to just know what to do or buy.

All you need to do is write to me (or any Masonic book publisher) and you can help on how to get quality books. With just a little effort you can be shown how to get the most for your dollar or your lodge's dollar. But you must act.

Just What is Important in Freemasonry?

A few years ago, I visited a lodge that was always friendly and welcoming in its nature. Every time I went there, I was greeted with smiles, handshakes, and kind words. After saying hello to everyone, I went to the kitchen and returned with a plate of hot food. The meal before lodge looked good. I headed to a table where I saw an empty chair. As I was sitting down, I heard something that I did not often hear in this lodge. The members at the table were having what seemed to be an almost heated discussion — an argument. I was surprised and listened for a while. The Brothers were sharing their opinions as to what they felt was the most important aspect in Freemasonry. One Brother explained that our ritual is the "backbone" or "heart" of Freemasonry. He said that a real danger to any lodge is when its officers are unable to properly perform even the short opening and closing ritual in the lodge. I couldn't disagree with him. He said that sloppy ritual projects a sloppy attitude towards all aspects of the lodge. A lack of care in this visible portion of lodge operation invites a lack of caring in all aspects of the lodge. He pointed out that many lodges offer little more than this short ritual and a reading of the minutes. When they cannot even accomplish this small task, the lodge would seem to be able to offer very little of any substance to the members or visitors. I sat back and waited to hear how anyone could disagree with him.

A second Brother began speaking. He said that his point seemed to be lost by the first Brother. He said that even when ritual is perfectly done, it is, at best, only a performance. In itself, he said, the ritual is only a collection of words. A recording of a perfectly executed ritual could be played for the opening and closing of the lodge, and it would satisfy the need for a properly delivered ritual. He said that what he saw as the real danger is when the ritual is not understood. He recounted of his once asking a very good ritualist what the words he was saying meant. The ritualist knew the words, but not the meanings of the symbolic words or lessons delivered. He said that if we only perfectly repeat words that have no meaning to us, then our ritual only becomes something that we do, and it has no other benefit or meaning to us. It is only an empty and meaningless performance for our entertainment. I certainly could not disagree with him either. He went on to say that the philosophy of Freemasonry must be understood if we are to truly understand why the symbolic ritual is important. Without instruction in our philosophy and symbols, our ritual becomes pointless, and we mislead ourselves as to the importance of perfectly performed ritual. I found value in all that he said.

A third Brother said that he understood the points and logic of the two other Brothers, but he felt that our true danger was repeating the failures of the past. He said that we must know our history. When we do not know of past failures, and what caused them, the opportunity is present to travel down the same problematic roads that brought us previous difficulty. He said that knowledge of our history gives us a window into our past and provides us with a blueprint of sorts to explore the future and what we need to avoid. Once again, I found no fault in what this brother was saying.

An elderly brother then came out of the kitchen. He had been listening as well. He mentioned that they left out one additional point that he felt was essential. He pointed out that all Masons must know our Masonic rules and regulations. If we don't know our laws, then we are far more likely to make mistakes that could bring us serious, unforeseen problems. But what he felt was *most* important is that we do not divide our area of study into only history, ritual, philosophy, or anything else. He said that no one aspect of Freemasonry was better or more important than another. Balance is essential to Freemasonry. We must be able to properly function in *all* areas of Masonry if we are to properly consider ourselves a MASTER Mason.

It is not a matter of which is more important. It is a matter of recognizing that all areas are important and in need of study. We should objectively examine ourselves to find our weak spots and do the work necessary to improve in Masonry wherever needed. It is true that if we look at our teachings in the proper manner, we will be taking advantage of all the teachings for all of our lives. The learning and growing will never cease.

The Five to Ten Minute Masonic Lecture

Over the last few years, I've heard opinions from a few brothers about blanket time limits for educational talks. I've heard that those attending such talks have a time limit of, at most, between five, ten, or fifteen minutes before interest is lost. I've also read a few published studies that seem to support such thoughts. A few times I've been invited to speak somewhere, and the Worshipful Master will ask me in advance to keep the talk down to about ten minutes — at the longest. I've even heard a few speaking loudly around me saying how "everyone knows" that a speaker loses his audience after ten about minutes. The suggestion is that this is a hard and fast rule for any Masonic lecture. If any talk goes beyond ten or fifteen minutes, then the thought is that it's not an appreciated or valued talk. Masons will lose interest. It becomes an unwanted intrusion in their Masonic experience rather than help.

I've done a good bit of thinking on this opinion of lecture lengths and have some thoughts on the subject.

I remember my school days. High school was far different than college. I had no choice but to sit in my high school classes and listen to whatever lecture was being presented. I suffered through most all of it. Many times, it did not take five or ten minutes for me to lose attention — I could be off somewhere in space after only a minute or two! So very many times, I had little to no interest in what was being presented. I simply had to sit there and go through it if I wanted to pass the class and not have to repeat the torture. While college did offer me more freedom, and it was not required by law that I attend, I still felt that same trapped feeling if an instructor droned on about some subject that held no interest for me. Not every instructor was an interesting speaker and not every class that I was required to take for my major was of great interest to me. So, if the speaking skill of the instructor was limited or if the subject was of little interest to me, then I can very well see this five or ten minute rule as valid and factual.

But what about other subjects? What about comedy, for example? I could sit there and listen to a good stand-up comedian for an hour and a half and not once lose interest in anything that was said. I would laugh my head off the whole time. I would be giving any good comedian my full attention and when it was over, I often wished that it would go on longer. Under these conditions, this attention span time limit is nonsense. A good movie or TV show could also hold my full attention for far longer than five or ten minutes.

But let's go back to college. I do remember one instructor who was outstanding. I had been advised to take his class as I was told I would enjoy every minute of it. They were right. He was a history professor and he truly made history come to life for me. The fact is that I enjoyed history and his manner and style of speaking not only held my attention but made his lectures a truly enjoyable event. But then again, others may have no interest at all in history and find it tiresome to listen to lectures about it. See where this is going?

This attention span theory of five to ten minutes seems to be sound if you are indifferent or have little to no interest in the subject, or if the instructor or speaker is of only limited ability. Humans always love entertainment. In the Middle-Ages a good storyteller was constantly in high demand and crowds would listen to them all day if allowed. If a speaker entertains you by his manner and style of speech or if by what he is saying, then this five or ten minute rule flies out the window. We can listen all day to something that is of interest to us. So, how does all this apply to Freemasonry?

Without trying to offend anyone (although I probably will), some Masons seek only fellowship, a hot meal, and the opportunity to show everyone how important they are in Masonry. They have no real interest in learning or exploring any of the deeper teachings of Freemasonry. Their interest in Masonry seems to exist elsewhere. A lecture on any of the deeper aspects of Masonic philosophy or symbolism might be of no real interest to them. It is an intrusion into whatever else they could be doing. After five or ten minutes listening to anyone speaking on the symbolism of Freemasonry, they might well be twisting in their chairs looking for a way to get out. On the other hand, others listening to the same lecture may be fixed on every word of the speaker, totally captivated by the subject. It all depends on our interest. It also depends on what we want out of the Masonic experience.

So, what do we do? How to we satisfy the hunger for some while not boring others to tears? Is there a middle ground?

I believe that several factors need to come into play or be put into play. The first is that we need to be completely honest and open with ourselves. If we have a desire to learn more about Freemasonry, we can't let anything stop us. If we have no desire to learn anything more about Freemasonry, we can't allow ourselves to be pushed into it. But in neither case can we push our wants or needs on anyone else. We must follow our own paths without expecting anyone else to join us. We need to find and live the style of Masonry that interests us and not allow peer pressure to influence us. If you seek Masonic education, then go out and find it. It is possible. If your lodge, or vocal members of your lodge, will not tolerate Masonic lectures of substance, then you can find them in books and online videos. If you just attend lodge for the social aspects, then don't go on nights that have educational programs that may hold no interest for you. If you do go, have the politeness to not show your displeasure and make the evening unpleasant for those who do find value in the event. In either case, don't insult or be a pain to those who do not share your opinion or view of Freemasonry. If an event or even if your lodge no longer suits you, find another. Don't fall for the nonsense that you owe loyalty to something that is not going in the direction where you want to go.

But, on a technical point, it is very possible that there is value in, and a need for, a five to ten minute talk. Let's say that a lodge has a very full business meeting where some issues simply cannot be handled before or after the lodge. Let's say that you only have a few minutes extra and you would like it to be on some aspect of education. It is very possible to give a useful and interesting talk in that amount of time. Not every good Masonic talk has to be complex and lengthy. For example, if you select one working tool and talk on only one aspect of the symbolism of it, this is something that can be done within those time limits. This is different from cutting short a Masonic lecture because of a lack of interest in the subject, it is planning a short talk due to a full agenda. There is a time and a place for everything.

So, it seems that like everything else, balance comes into play. There is value and use for a short talk on Freemasonry. It doesn't have to be an excuse for not desiring good Masonic education. It all depends on what we want out of Freemasonry. I believe that by sincere members working together, we can find an acceptable middle ground for everyone.

The Five to Ten Minute Masonic Lecture

I have enjoyed many short talks that I have heard in lodge. I have also enjoyed longer talks where some subject was explored in greater detail than could be done in a short talk.

I have also heard short talks that were clearly originally longer talks that was chopped down to turn them into short talks. These are usually disjointed and not of the quality that they might have been in their original state. I normally leave such talks disappointed.

The quality and value of a lecture comes from its content, not its length.

Scottish Rite Questions and Answers

I received an email from a Scottish Rite Brother with three specific questions about the Scottish Rite.

The questions are:

#1. *Which is the older, the Scottish Rite or the York Rite?*
#2. *What's the difference between the Scottish Rite and York Rite?*
#3. *If someone is a member of the York Rite, why do they need to join the Scottish Rite?*

Let's start with the first question. Which is the older, the Scottish Rite or the York Rite?

When we talk about the age of any Masonic Rite, it can very easily turn into a trick question. I don't mean to suggest that the one asking the question is playing games, but the one asking the question may be thinking one thing and the one answering may be thinking of something else. As an example, let's look at something outside of Masonry.

Let's say that someone is in charge of a kid's summer camp and is planning meals. He is aware that some of the kids have food restrictions, and he doesn't want to serve anything that is any sort of problem for any of the campers. So, he posts what he believes is a clever way of obtaining the needed information. He asks: *What two things do you never eat for breakfast?* One of the kids answers with: *lunch and dinner.* Well, he's right (and maybe a bit cleverer than the camp counselor), but that didn't give the information that was needed.

The Particular Nature of Freemasonry

Masonic rites have a perceived dual nature. The rites are often viewed as both the organization and the ritual. When you ask about the age of Scottish Rite, it can mean the organization or the ritual. They do have different ages. This is where things can start to get very confusing.

I want to proceed carefully here as just one wrong or confusing turn can lead someone down a very wrong path, as many, many others have gone down. It is one of the reasons why our history is a mess.

The organization date of the *Scottish Rite* (meaning the 33-degree system) is 1801. It was created in Charleston, South Carolina.

The York Rite in the United States is often understood as the unique collection of degrees and bodies following the craft lodge that end with the degree of Knights Templar. The organization date of the York Rite (meaning the finalization of the accepted collection of bodies and rituals) was about 1816 (and that's a few years this way or that depending on who you ask). It is also the date of several national Masonic conventions in the U.S. and the recognized date of the founding of the Grand Encampment.

So, the answer would seem to be that the Scottish Rite is the older. But there are those who will debate that statement. In fact, Albert Mackey is one of the ones who disagrees with my opinion of who is older.

In his *Encyclopedia of Freemasonry*, Mackey very clearly states that the "York Rite" is the "oldest of the Masonic Rites."[1] He then goes on to support that statement by tracing the York Rite back through its craft degrees and then back to Masonry's early days in Great Britain. That's what I mean by a trick question and answer.

We can talk about the age of an organization. We can talk about the age of a particular ritual (meaning when the ritual was written). We can also talk about the age of systems, bodies or rituals that inspired, or from which later rituals or organizations trace themselves. But, if we jumble them all together then we can very well come up with an answer that sounds right but is, at best, misleading.

When we talk about the age of a Masonic organization, we must limit ourselves to *only* the organization in question. For clarity, Mackey should have only dealt with the bodies that are commonly known as "The York Rite" — meaning from the 4th degree onward. Mackey should not have sought to connect older bodies or rituals that were not (and are not) part of this unique system known in the U.S. as the York Rite. But the same can be done (and has been done) with the Scottish Rite.

When tracing the dates of various Scottish Rite bodies, we often find different Scottish Rite bodies listing bodies existing prior to 1801 in their linage. The problem is that these pre-1801 bodies are mostly the old *Order of the Royal Secret*, also known as *The Rite of Perfection*. That's a different system. It's not correct when trying to date an organization to bring into the mix older bodies that are not part of that system.

So, let's go over this again carefully.

If we talk about the two "main rites" in the US, then we are talking about the York Rite and the Scottish Rite. In the US Grand Lodge system, we have two organizations understood as being worked from the 4th degree onward. The craft lodge is considered something of a separate system. Before anyone writes to me, I know that they are not, but it is how they are *commonly viewed* in the US.

What we *call* the York Rite and the Scottish Rite *both* are commonly understood in the US as beginning on the 4th degree. This is why so many of our Masonic charts list both of these rites as *appendant bodies* which begin *after* the craft lodge. Yes, it's wrong, but that's for another discussion.

So, let's again look at the age of the two *organizations* in the US known as the Scottish Rite and the York Rite. First, we need to set some ground rules. We will now talk about two organizations which were created in the United States. We will not deal with any rituals or with organizations which might have inspired or lead to the creations of either of these bodies. The two bodies are known as the York Rite and the Scottish Rite.

The organization date of the Scottish Rite is 1801. There are many documents to support that date.

The unique US organization that we call the York Rite was created about 1816. It is what Albert Mackey renamed, "The American Rite." That name unfortunately didn't stick. I wish it had stuck.

So, by these dates the Scottish Rite is older. Simple — or is it? If it's simple, then why does there seem to be so much debate and confusion? Is the date or the age of a Masonic rite really that important? Well, yes and no.

No, as far as symbolic value, educational importance, or Masonic significance, it is *not* important which organization is a handful of years older. But, yes, as far as bragging rights are concerned, it's very important. Who is older is important for no other reason than to make the big shots in either organization feel a bit more important.

In fact, without much effort, we can find official looking documents for various York Rite bodies as well as Scottish Rite bodies where they both trace themselves back to far earlier dates than the ones I gave. They also give the names, dates, and locations of older bodies — inside and outside of the US!

How can that be explained?

It can be explained because we are talking about different organizations and different bodies. In addition, we sometimes incorrectly connect bodies to older ones through rituals that are the same or very similar to the ones used by older bodies. This is part of the trap into which we can fall. I believe that many who are writing these incorrect things do not even know that they are in error.

Let's look at what this all means.

What we today call the *Scottish Rite* was created as a 33-degree system in 1801 in Charleston, South Carolina. The guys who created this organization did *not* sit down and write all new rituals for this new organization. They took older rituals and modified them as they liked and placed them in the order that they liked. Bingo! It became known as the Ancient and Accepted Scottish Rite.

This was exactly what was done with the York Rite. The ones in the US who put together the organization, sat down and created this unique American system by using and sometimes editing older rituals to create what they called the York Rite.

The creators invented these new organizations by taking older rituals, editing them as they desired and using them to create something new. If we pull out one of the Scottish Rite rituals and trace it back to 1740 in France and then one York Rite ritual and trace it back without question to 1735 in England, does that mean that the York Rite is older than the Scottish Rite? No, and for the very reasons that I have already given.

The creation date of an organization does not necessarily match the creation date of the ritual used by that organization. New organizations were created with older rituals. Of course, if we are talking about *only* rituals, and not the organizations, and we trace them back as far as we can, then can we determine which is older, the York Rite or the Scottish Rite? Actually, I believe that we can.

If we look at it that way, then they are both the same age. The reason I say this is because the rituals of the Scottish Rite can be traced back to France. French Masonic rituals came to France from Great Britain. The York right traces itself back to England. The argument can be reasonably made that both systems trace themselves back to pretty much the same time and place — or they become so tangled and lost in details and history that nothing can be completely proven. The slight differences of date (even if able to be proven) becomes irrelevant and all but impossible to completely prove. The age question becomes as unimportant and debatable as the question of which came first, the chicken or the egg.

On to the second question. What's the difference between the Scottish Rite and York Rite?

The Scottish Rite is more French in "flavor" and the York Rite more English. When Masonry arrived in France, they faced a problem of language. They needed to translate the ritual into French if there was any hope of having it widely accepted. The unknown translator or translators not only translated the ritual from English into French, but they considered the French culture. The French ritual became more dramatic, theatrical, and openly alchemical. The ritual was edited in a way to appeal more to the French people.

While the 33-degree organization that we know today as the Scottish Rite is an American creation, its rituals have their roots in France and carry the same French flavor. While what we call the York Rite is also an American invention, its roots are in Great Britain and carry much of that flavor.

Both the York Rite and Scottish Rite are Templar in nature, both are esoteric, and both teach lessons of honor, duty, integrity, and much more. Both are of obvious value and clearly Masonic, but each takes you down a path of their own creation. The two rites have a different number of degrees, they organize themselves differently, and have different structures.

There are books that can give an idea of the feel of both rites and any good Masonic encyclopedia can give you enough details on the two rites to provide a basic understanding of the nature and practices of the two systems. I can't get into the actual ritual here, nor do I believe it would be beneficial to get into details of the officer and governmental structure of the two systems. I can clearly tell you that the two systems are not duplications of the same system. Both are obviously Masonic, but are very different from each other in ritual, structure, and practice.

And I guess that does lead us into the final question of why someone who is a member of the York Rite might "need" to join the Scottish Rite?

Let me first say this. The concept that we would "need" to join something disturbs me as it can take on an almost sinister interpretation. It is sometimes associated with the club mentality at its lowest form.

I have personally heard Masons tell other Masons, *"If you want to have any hope of getting **this** prize, then you need to join this body."* I've heard it used applying to both the York Rite and Scottish Rite. Some view belonging to certain bodies as a necessary springboard for invitational bodies or becoming a "big shot." It is disturbing to me.

But, of course, for many years the need to belong to *something else* applied to the Shriners. If you wanted to join the Shrine, then you needed to first join either the York Rite or the Scottish Rite. It was a prerequisite.

But I've heard this "joining something else" concept in other situations as well. I once heard a 33rd going from table to table at a Scottish Rite Reunion where all the new candidates were sitting and telling each table that if they wanted to be able to truly complete and understand the Scottish Rite then they would need to join the York Rite (he was more of a "big wig" in the York Rite). I spoke about this in another paper. It is 100% false.

The Scottish Rite and York Rite are both complete systems of Freemasonry that do not depend on each other for completion of their own systems. One does not need to join either the York Rite or the Scottish Rite unless they want to be in the York Rite and/or the Scottish Rite.

But maybe the question is really, if I am a member of the York Rite, why would I be interested in joining the Scottish Rite? This is certainly not the first time that this question has come up and I am frankly just as puzzled now as I was the first time that I heard it. It's like asking the question, why would I go to this restaurant when I am already a customer of another restaurant? Even if I have no complaints whatsoever about one restaurant, I still want to try others. I enjoy good food and I like finding it in any number of good restaurants. Likewise, I enjoy the symbolic Masonic education available in the various Masonic rites.

I enjoy the wisdom of Freemasonry. I enjoy thinking about the lessons taught in the various bodies, how they may apply to my life, and how I can use them to help me improve myself. Yes, both the York Rite and the Scottish Rite teach the basic lessons of Freemasonry, but they are different. Each system takes certain moral lessons and offers them in their own unique fashion.

Of course, what if I hear that a restaurant has a horrible reputation, serves bad food, has rude waiters and waitresses, and charges far too much for what they deliver? Well, I most likely will give that restaurant a miss. But that's different than just not experiencing other restaurants because you like the one you normally visit.

The sad truth is that there are certain York Rite and Scottish Rite bodies that drop the ball and provide nothing in the way of real Masonic education. If the membership in these bodies want nothing but a hot meal and visiting with friends, then it's fine. But these bodies reflect sometimes on the whole of the rite and can make others believe that this is the way the whole rite operates. I've seen this with both the York Rite and Scottish Rite.

The Scottish Rite and the York Rite are beautiful systems of Freemasonry. Each has lessons upon lessons that are of benefit to all. Each has a unique manner of symbolic instruction that retenders neither unnecessary. Joining the Scottish Rite does not duplicate the lessons or teachings of the York Rite. Neither rite completes the other nor provides unnecessary repetition of the other system. It is very true that one rite may be far more appealing to some Masons, but this is normal and why it is of benefit to have more than one Masonic rite available.

We are all different and are following different Masonic paths. There is no shame, dishonor, or lack of loyalty for following the path that suits you best — or following both paths. It is one of the beauties of Freemasonry.

Notes:

1. Albert Mackey, Revised William J. Hughan, Edward L. Hawkins *An Encyclopedia of Freemasonry* (New York: The Masonic History Company, 1927), Vol. II 871.

"We Meet Upon the Level"

When I first joined Freemasonry, I was deeply moved by the philosophy and moral lessons that were taught in the ritual and monitors. But what moved me the most was that so much of the teachings were layered. By that I mean, the lessons were presented in a way that if you wished to only consider the outer teachings, that was fine. But, if you wanted to dig deeper, there was so much more to discover. For me, this was the true beauty of Freemasonry. You could custom tailor the teachings for each individual. You could go as far as your ability and interest took you.

But then we came to the part where we spoke of the level, and how we all "meet upon the level." The clear message being sent was that we were all equal. All the members of the lodge were on the same "level." That sounds nice, but it's just not true.

Some years back, I revised the classic *Robert's Rules of Order* into a Masonic edition. As was pointed out in the revised edition, the office of Worshipful Master has far greater rights, authority, and power than the presiding officers of clubs. It's one of the reasons why the classic, unrevised edition of *Roberts Rules of Order* is so problematic for a Masonic lodge. The membership of a lodge is simply not equal in authority to the Worshipful Master.

In fact, in society we are not all equal. We most certainly have equal value as human beings, but we all have different abilities, skills, and levels of knowledge. One person may be good at singing, another at building things, or art, or science, or on and on. We all have some things that we are good at and some things at which we are not so good. If we were all equal, we would be photocopies, or clones, of each other. That's not the case. We are all individually distinct human beings.

So, what do we mean when we say that we are all "upon the level"? If you stop and think about our degrees, teachings, and rituals, you will see that we provide the same rituals and teachings to all our candidates. Yes, each jurisdiction is a little different and the rituals vary a little to a lot. But the basic elements of initiation and the story line are the same no matter the ritual, rite, or jurisdiction. We all teach the Hiramic Legend. Maybe it is a little different from jurisdiction to jurisdiction, but the basic elements are the same.

All candidates and initiates are given the same basic symbolic tools and opportunities. All candidates are given the same message through the degrees: *"Here are symbolic working tools that you can, if you choose, make use of to create improvements in yourself."* The choice of taking advantage of the teachings and lessons is always 100% up to the initiates. No one is going to force anyone to grow, advance, or be anything that they do not choose to be.

When we say that we are all on the level, it doesn't mean that we have identical skills, talents, strengths, or weaknesses. It also does not mean that we are required to learn at the same speed or that we must participate in all the teachings.

In the days of the old Operative Freemasons, they used the level as an actual working tool for their profession. It was used to assure that theirs was quality work. The old Operatives earned their livings by the value of the work that they did.

Proper use of their tools assured them that they would continue to work.

In Speculative Freemasonry it's not required that we take advantage of the symbolic lessons that we are given. We will not be fired from our Masonry if we do not grow because of the lessons that we are given. We can just sit back in lodge and enjoy the show.

While sitting back, failing to grow, and basically doing nothing but being there would have resulted in an Operative Mason being thrown out of the lodge, the same is not true with us. In fact, just sitting there, or being there, in some lodges can result in your election to become a lodge leader. That's the *real* trouble with some lodges. We are simply not all equal in ability, skill, and performance. If the only ability that the lodge needs for its leadership positions is the ability to show up, then the lodge is in far more danger than it realizes.

The symbol of the level teaches that we all have the same value as human beings. It doesn't matter as to our skill set, any abilities that we may, or may not have, or the level of our personal growth because of the lessons we are given. As a human being, we are all due equal respect, fair treatment, and basic decency. But the lodge is also due the very same things. We must be fair and respectful to the lodge as well as the members. If one member is very good at ritual and your close friend is horrible at ritual, do you pick your friend as the lodge ritualist because we are all on the level?

Being on the level means only that we are all given the same lessons and opportunity to gain experience and grow. We are all valued, respected, and treated the same. Being on the level does not mean that we are all assumed to instantly possess the same abilities, skills, or experiences. Being fair does not mean that we get what we want simply because we want it.

The lessons of Freemasonry require study and often restudy. We grow in Masonry because of the work we put into our study. The best lesson that we can take away from this aspect of Masonic philosophy is that we need to be dead honest with ourselves about ourselves. We are not to allow that little green devil known as envy to force us to focus on others who may have different, or greater, talents in certain areas than us. We *all* have our own unique talents — discovered or undiscovered. We are to focus on ourselves and the work that we need to do to reach our own full potential. We are in competition with only ourselves.

A lodge is to treat all its members with equal fairness and respect. However, we must remember that lodge (or Grand Lodge) leadership must be based on whoever is the best qualified. Fairness to the organization is just as important as fairness to the individual.

Should Masons be Allowed to Smoke, Eat, or Drink in Open Lodge?

No. No one should smoke, eat, or drink in an open lodge. OK, the paper is ended, right? Well, probably not. There are going to be some who claim that exceptions can be made. There will be some who say that the Worshipful Master makes the rules in a lodge. But really, why would eating or drinking in lodge be a problem? Everyone eats and if we clean up our mess, why should it be a problem? But it doesn't feel exactly right. It is almost a vague or nagging, intuitive feeling that it is something that we should not do. It *feels* that we should eat in certain places, but not in others. Let's look a bit at where, when, and how we have been taught to eat.

Let's get smoking out of the way quickly. Most public buildings today have laws concerning smoking. Smoking is recognized as a public health risk. Many still smoke, but most all recognize that it is a habit that can and does kill. It is not a matter of courtesy to refrain from smoking in lodges, it is a law in most all areas. But what about eating and drinking?

Socrates is often quoted as saying, *"Thou shouldst eat to live; not live to eat."* Since the dawn of mankind, humans have viewed eating as something more than just an act of survival. We have developed often complex rules, customs, traditions, rituals, and even taboos about eating. Humans are social, so we like to eat with others. Humans prefer the taste of some foods over others. We have developed social customs based on preferences in certain areas. This group may like this, and that group likes something else. Traditions and customs relating to eating may have started by someone getting sick after eating something or just enjoying it. Some customs are local and others worldwide. Some customs make sense; others seem random.

Food taboos are often localized or associated with various religions or social beliefs. Judaism and Muslim faiths often forbid the eating of pork while Hinduism forbids the eating of beef. Most Western countries disapprove of eating dog or cat meat, yet other parts of the world find eating these animals completely acceptable. Nearly every culture finds the eating of other humans (cannibalism) absolutely and morally unacceptable. Over time, different types of mammals, birds, seafood, insects, and reptiles have been considered acceptable or unacceptable to eat. But it is not just meat that can be a problem. Eating the wrong plant can kill you — or at least, make you deathly sick. Animals seem to know instinctively which plants they should and which they should not eat. Humans, on the other hand, seem less connected with nature. We have far greater intelligence (at least, that's our claim), but what we eat seems far more connected with customs learned from our family or general biases that come from our society or personal choices. Our connection to the world around us is most often superficial. And yet, our senses do play a role in food selection. The smell, color, and appearance of a food guides us in our deciding if we want to try and eat something or not.

Socrates knew of the dangers of eating for pleasure. But eating for pleasure was normally reserved through much of history for the wealthy nobility. While the rich enjoyed elaborate banquet tables filled with every imaginable type of food, most of the people in early times were poor. They normally ate one meal a day until around the 1700s. The concept of three "square meals" a day is a relatively recent invention.

The poor in the Middle Ages ate pretty much whatever they grew or could afford to buy. Meals often consisted of eggs, cabbage, grains, and dark bread. Ale or mead was normally the drink of the adults and milk for the children. Every few days, they might have some fish (if they lived near a river or other body of water), cheese, poultry, or bacon. Hunting was often outlawed. Wild game or select meat was often considered reserved for the royals or the wealthy. Honey, herbs, roots, nuts, and various wildflowers were also eaten as well as used in health tonics.

Dining practices and what were used for eating are also historically different from today. A spoon and knife can be traced to early times. Knives had many survival uses for early man. Spoons soon followed for eating hot soups and broths. Forks were a relatively later invention and were originally a two-prong tool for stabbing meat on a plate. Hands were normally used in eating in a manner that would likely be considered today as unacceptable for "polite dining." A piece of meat would be cut into a manageable size and then picked up to be eaten. Because of the way the hands were used in eating, a meal could be a messy, and noisy, endeavor.

This all brings us to where we eat. Certainly, humans have eaten next to campfires under the stars. Many claim today that there are health benefits from picnicking. It's said that eating outdoors reduces stress. I imagine that if you picnic in a beautiful area by a lake or flowing stream, then you would feel better in such a setting. It makes sense. But what about eating indoors?

Our home is our castle. It has never mattered if a home was only one or two rooms. Eating in one's home has always provided a sense of comfort and security. It is where many to most eat their meals. We come in from the outside world and feel some sense of relaxation by simply being home. Yes, in today's fast paced world, many grab a burger and eat it in the car on the way to some meeting. But most everyone, if given a choice between fast food or a home cooked meal, will choose the home. I've found no record of there ever being any issues in any culture with eating, drinking, or smoking inside one's own home. But, what about food and eating in public or private buildings?

Ever since the terror attacks of 9/11, much has changed for anyone entering any government building or airport. If you carry a pocketknife (as my father and grand-father *always* did), don't even think about going into these places while it is in your pocket. Your choice is to leave your knife at home, in your car, or you can give it to the guards. But the same is true of packaged food or drinks. Once you pass through security, you can buy food and beverages, but you are not allowed to bring anything in with you. But once inside the buildings, there does not seem to be a hard and fast rule in most places concerning where you eat the food. But there are exceptions.

Years ago, I served on a jury for a murder trial. Prior to the trial, all the perspective jurors were sitting in the court room answering questions from the attorneys. The guy sitting next to me reached in his pocket and pulled out a small packet of peanuts. He opened the packet and started munching on the nuts. As best as I can remember, actual flames came out of the eyes of the judge when he noticed what he was doing. It was not a good day for the peanut lover. I learned then that eating in a court room was not allowed.

Depending on your faith, eating in church might bring about serious frowns. Even in the very early days, the idea of eating in a House of Worship was not well looked upon. From the Bible:

> *"Don't you have homes to eat and drink in? Or do you despise the church of God by humiliating those who have nothing? What shall I say to you? Shall I praise you? Certainly not in this matter!"*
>
> (1 Corinthians 11:22 NIV)

Since the beginning of time, there have been do's and don'ts for eating. But it's not only humans. Even the animal kingdom has rules for eating. In the wild, the alpha male is many times the first to eat his fill of a fresh kill. In some cultures, it is the oldest male who eats first out of respect for him. Other cultures will have the mother, or oldest female, eat or served first. Many times, we do not end up exactly neat and tidy after a meal (especially if it is one where the hands are used, like pizza or fried chicken). In such cases, eating in any place that is considered special for any reason at all is often considered inappropriate. Even for only the reason that we would not want to cause a mess through spills. It is not usually a law, but it's not done by most.

When a lodge is at labor, the Bible is open on the Altar. Yes, Freemasonry is not a religion, but we are still talking about the Bible. What we do in lodge is something that we represent as important. If the officers are sipping drinks and various members of the lodge are snacking on candy bars or whatever, then some of the dignity due the lodge can rightly be assumed to be lost. In some cultures, eating was a time for relaxing. Diners would lounge back and enjoy their meal in as near total relaxation as possible. Much of what we do, and don't do in Masonry is in memory of long-lost days. We should not lounge around in a lodge at labor. Showing respect for an important place, like a lodge room, requires doing and not doing certain things. We may have forgotten old customs concerning the lodge, but that does not mean that they are unimportant.

I don't know if we will see many jurisdictions having actual laws about eating in lodges, but out of respect for the institution, or even just concern for creating a mess, I will avoid it. It's not something that I would consider doing. Meals can be eaten in a dining hall, and if you did not get enough to eat, remain in the dining area until you are full. Don't bring the last bits of your meal to finish off in the lodge. I believe that the lodge should be reserved for philosophical and moral teachings. Eat your Snickers bar outside of the lodge. Yes, we all have freedoms, but we should also have some manners.

Masonic Dirty Laundry

There are those who seem to be determined to find fault with Freemasonry. Nothing about our Fraternity is good. It sometimes turns into the life work of some of the more feverous anti-Masons, although some of these are in reality anti-Masonic businessmen trying to make a few dollars by telling known falsehoods about the Fraternity.

One claim made by more than a few anti-Masons is that Freemasonry is a *secret* society. It is usually said or written with a sinister overtone, implying evil doing on our part and our desire to keep secret all kinds of foul deeds. It's a no-win trap. If we deny their charges and say that we are not a *secret* society, but only a "society with secrets," then they yell that we are playing word games. They will demand that we tell them everything concerning rituals, obligations, and modes of recognition. If we refuse, then we confirm (by their logic) that we are as they claim.

I've read a few Masonic papers suggesting that we stop allowing the anti-Masons to write the narrative and embrace the idea that we are, indeed, a *secret society*. I tend to agree with these Masonic authors. Those who wish to think poorly of us will do so no matter what we say or how we define ourselves. The fact is that we do have ceremonies that we do not make available to anyone who is not "one of us." Calling these "secrets" is fair. Taking that to the next level and saying that anything that is unknown to everyone is evil is *not* fair, but it is just how these types operate. They are what they are.

But this brings us to the point of this paper, exactly what is a Masonic secret, and I mean beyond what we normally understand as secrets? Should our Minutes, our bank account numbers, or the social security numbers of all our members be available to anyone who asks? What is the difference between *private* and *secret*? Are we obligated to do whatever anyone wants under the threat of their speaking falsehoods about us? Truthfully, I don't care what nuts think or say about us. I take an extremely dim view of handing blackmailers any control over us.

But what are members entitled to know about our own organization? I once heard a lodge treasurer say that the lodge is not entitled to know all that exists about the lodge finances as they would probably not understand and cause problems in the smooth running of the business end of the lodge. I find this way of thinking insulting and disturbing. A treasurer needs to report to the lodge as often as the lodge says that he needs to report. If he does not want to do this, then the lodge needs a new treasurer. Neither individual officers nor little groups can withhold important information about the lodge from the lodge members. The lodge belongs to the members.

Because lodge secretaries and treasurers often hold office for sometimes many years, they can at times let the job go to their head. All officers must remember that they hold office to serve, not to feed their ego. The members of a lodge are not outsiders. They are fully entitled to know all the details of the functioning of the lodge.

The flip side of the coin is that the business of the lodge is the business of the lodge. Those who are not members of a lodge do not have the right to demand information about the lodge operation — Grand Lodge excepted. The Worshipful Master of a lodge is fully within his rights to announce that the business of the lodge is to remain within the lodge. Such a statement must be with the understanding that this would include the Grand Lodge. If a Worshipful Master would announce that the Grand Lodge is not to be told of anything going on within the lodge, then this is the cue for every thinking member of that lodge to report such statements to the District Deputy.

Privacy regarding the business of a lodge is a serious matter and is not for the inexperienced. It is one of the reasons why brand-new Masons should not be run through the chairs of the lodge. If a charge is made against a member of the lodge, it needs to be investigated. A charge is not a conviction. Many charges are not considered as they lack any fact at all or are shown to be simply disagreements with no violation of Masonic law at all. But, if a charge is made and then one who learns of it starts spreading around that brother so-and-so did this or that, then he could be the next one facing Masonic charges. We must know how to be discreet in all matters of Masonic business.

What to say and what not to say in regard to Masonic trials is something that can vary from Grand Lodge to Grand Lodge. In the days of the old Operative Masons, one who violated any law was usually openly and loudly thrown out of the group. The Operatives wanted everyone to know that this guy was *not* one of them any longer because of his actions. Their work depended on their reputation, so they would make clear examples of anyone who might tarnish their reputation. Modern Grand Lodges working as Speculative Masons operate differently. Some Grand Lodges feel the need to keep Masonic trials private. In such cases, only certain Grand Lodge officers will know details of the trials. Other Grand Lodges operate with a variety of different levels of transparency.

Intent is always important when trying to understand why something happened. It is possible that poor judgment resulted in someone talking about a Mason losing his job, or his wife leaving him, or any personal matter. But, if it is simply a lack of care about the feelings of a brother, then this is a very sad commentary on Freemasons today. We must have the wisdom and awareness of the feelings of others to guard our words and keep private the matters of others. Even if a brother does not come out and say that what he is saying to us is private, we must use discretion. We must have the sensitivity and understanding to realize what would be painful if spread around. We need to use common sense. If we do not show good judgment with our brothers, then we can hardly claim to have benefitted from any of the lessons of Freemasonry.

As with so many things, we need to find a balance with all aspects of "dirty laundry" in Masonry. Yes, some will try to find (or make up) terrible things to try and show that we are one step away from Hell's Gate. Ignore them. But some Masons will speak out of turn on sensitive matters concerning individual Masons, lodges, and even Grand Lodges. Other Masons will try to keep silent about lodge matters that should be available to lodge members. In all these things, our answers are found in what we teach. Light brought to falsehoods, ill deeds, or cries for guidance will ultimately bring good.

Do We Need Masonic Charity?

A Mason spoke with me not long ago about something I had written a while back. I had mentioned that Freemasonry is not a club. It's not a social, civil, or charitable club. He said that if charity has no role in Freemasonry, then why does it seem important in our ritual. I pointed out that there is a difference between being charitable and being a charitable club or organization. It also dawned on me that the whole concept of charity might need to be revisited.

To start with, Freemasonry is both a philosophy and an organization. Our philosophy is the symbolic lessons designed to take someone who is basically good and help them make improvements in their lives. The philosophy of Freemasonry exists apart from the organization of Freemasonry, but it is a vital part of the organization. Without the philosophy of Freemasonry, the organization does, indeed, become a club.

Charity is one of the philosophical lessons of Masonry. But Freemasonry itself is not a charitable organization or club. We have a different role. Professional charitable organizations such as the United Way, Red Cross, Salvation Army, Habitat for Humanity, and many others exist to raise and distribute money and aid to those in need. That is their reason for existing. Freemasonry does not exist for the sole purpose of extending charity.

Having said the above, Freemasonry, or should I say, *Freemasons*, are known for extending charity when needed. But, just as there is some confusion as to if Freemasonry is a charitable organization, there is a misunderstanding about charity itself. I'd like to look a bit at the act of charity. There are times when charity might be of far less actual help than we might believe. It is this misunderstanding that may contribute to how some people (as well as some Masons) become confused as to Freemasonry's role in charity.

Those who need charity seem to fall into two categories — those who have just come into need and those who have been in need for some time. Right after a flood, hurricane, tornado, or some other disaster, there will be people in need of help. They were going along with their lives and out of the blue, something unexpected happened and everything was lost. They need help now. Charity towards them normally comes in the manner of food, temporary housing (if needed), and medical needs. Normally this type of need arises so quickly that most who extend charity do so without really thinking about it. This is also where any of the many professional charitable organizations shine. Meal wagons show up giving out hot food. Shelters open where the needy can sleep, have a shower and such. Community aid normally soon pops up. People in the area unaffected by the disaster donate extra clothing and food from their pantries. The immediate needs of the suffering are relieved, and they then can go about rebuilding their lives. But it is different for those who have been suffering for some time. The reality of long-term poverty and need can sometimes require a different kind of charity. Sometimes the "charity" that we give is more about us feeling good than bringing real help to the needy. Let me give you an example.

I watched a video about a celebrity who was being praised for his act of charity in giving food and aid to a small village in Africa. Apparently, he had seen the suffering taking place in numerous villages on TV. According to the report, he showed up in this village without notice bearing gifts. He flew into the village with a large supply of fast-food hamburgers in heated containers, bottles of water, and t-shirts. He tossed the t-shirts out to the crowd of happy waving villagers. He then passed out the hamburgers and water. Make no mistake, they truly were happy and appreciative of the gifts. The cameras showed the many smiling faces and the overall poverty of the village. The people felt good. The celebrity felt good, and the event was praised by all. But what was the real goal? Was the goal to truly help these people? If so, he may not have done as well as he may have believed or could have done.

Now, I don't want to seem to be throwing cold water on anyone, but I'd like to take a real, honest look at the needs and charity extended. Maybe something might have been missing. I'd like to reexamine the two examples of charity given above.

With any type of disaster, people are suddenly thrown into a state of immediate need. Maybe they required no aid the day before, but once the disaster happened, they were in real, serious trouble. Their normal lives were thrown upside down. Without aid, they may die because of the disaster. The gifts of food, clothing, and shelter were what was needed to help them. This type of charity holds people in this condition up while they can get their lives in order and rebuild. Because of the aid, they can return to their former lives, or near to it.

A poverty-stricken village is a different matter. Their crisis is having nothing at all. But the difference is that it did not happen all of a sudden. Their condition had existed for a long time. It is the reality of how they live. Bringing food and gifts to them did help them at the moment. But the very next day they will be hungry again. They would still be poor and in need. I'm sure that the celebrity had all good intentions. He saw images of very hungry people. He must have thought that he had money and he could go there and bring them some food. He acted out of kindness. But because he was not a professional charitable organization, he did not know how to provide the best kind of help in this situation.

The celebrity purchased burgers from somewhere for the village. He fed them for one day. Had he gone to the village ahead of time and spoken to the people there, maybe he could have taken that same money and bought some new tools and seed for the farmers. That would help feed the villagers for maybe several seasons. Maybe instead of investing in t-shirts, he could have given the money needed for a few medical supplies or equipment. Maybe he could have invested in something that could help their economy. The celebrity had a good heart, but because he was not in the business of charity, he did not fully understand the real needs.

Freemasonry is not a charitable organization. We are not trained in this type of aid and when we involve ourselves in any type of long-term aid to any in need, we can run into trouble. Yes, Freemasons can provide much needed help in times of disasters. I have seen photos of whole lodges going out to a stricken community helping with clean up or rebuilding after a disaster. But they are usually operating as individual Freemasons and under the direction of actual professionals working for charitable organizations.

We must understand that professional charitable organizations train their workers in the ways to provide the best assistance to individuals in need depending on the situation. They know what to do and are not sidetracked by the emotion of the situation. Freemasonry provides none of this training. We don't provide this training because we are not a charitable organization. When we try to take on the role of a charitable organization, and we are not trained in that field, then we can end up doing more harm than good. And that's even with the harm being done with all good intentions.

I saw a video clip of a TV actor that got himself in some trouble. He played a doctor on TV and went on a talk show and gave medical advice. He's an actor, not a doctor. Taking all the legal issues and putting them aside, he could have hurt someone by giving advice that sounded good to him but was medically incorrect. Freemasons are taught to help others on a personal basis and in a time of need. If we have no training, we can't assume the knowledge of trying to plan for meaningful aid to those in long term serious need. We, of course, can donate to those organizations who do this type of work. We can volunteer to feed the needy in a soup kitchen. We can do all kinds of things to help others. We can and should do these things. We simply cannot act as if we are something we are not.

"Know thyself."

Inscribed on the frontispiece of the Temple of Delphi.

A Growing Danger for Freemasonry

I'd like to write a bit about what seems to be a growing danger for Freemasonry. Really, it's a danger for all of society. It has to do with certain aspects of the media. It's truly a new world, and I believe that being informed is the best way to navigate potentially rocky times.

To begin with, when I use the term media, I won't be talking about only the various news outlets. In addition, I will be referring to advertisers and their practices as well as anyone who engages in these practices, including new technological gadgets and platforms that are being used in today's new world. I also want to point something out at the very start. Regardless of if I seem a bit harsh towards the various news outlets, this should not be taken as to mean that I am in favor of any sort of control over the news agencies.

Having a free and independent press is one of the hallmarks of democracy. It is very common for politicians to have rocky relationships with reporters. While it may be desired for reporters to act as a public relations service on the payroll of the politicians, it is the job of reporters to ask the hard, probing, and invasive questions. Even if the politicians feel they are being treated unfairly, they must be accountable to the public. It's how the public is able to judge politicians under pressure.

We must always remember that while the three branches of government are designed to be a check and balance for each other, the Free Press is an intricate part of democracy. It provides clear accountability of the government to the public. The failure of the Free Press to properly perform its duties does not mean that the Free Press must be eliminated, it only means that it must better understand its duty.

Another branch of the media is advertising. The goal of an advertising campaign is to convince the public to buy one product rather than another, even if they are essentially the same. Their job is to make the public want their product and believe that it is far better than other like products. They also, need to do so in as short a time as possible and with as few words as possible. There is no time for long explanations. They basically must tell the people what to do and when to do it.

A classic example of an ad campaign is a billboard sign on a highway. Drivers don't have the time to read any long explanation on signs. The billboard must be simple and able to be understood in a very short amount of time. Let's say that your client owns *Joe's Cafe*. A billboard on the highway might simply be an image of a large plate of nice-looking food with "*Eat at Joe's! Next Exit.*" You have clearly said what it is, where it is, and what to do. That's advertising.

Journalism, on the other hand, is the objective reporting of something that has happened or will happen. "*There was a fire at this building. No one was hurt. The building was a total loss.*" The job of a reporter is simply to report something to you.

Having worked in both journalism and advertising, I began to see a disturbing development. In order to pay bills, both newspapers and television stations include advertising departments. In the sometimes-heated struggle for advertising dollars, it became fiscally responsible, or so it seemed, for news to adopt some advertising techniques. The goal was to *juice up* the news a bit. If a station could acquire more viewers, then they could use that greater viewership as an incentive for advertisers to buy airtime with them rather than the competing TV stations with lesser viewers.

Little by little, the news began to tell not only what happened, but they began to give their opinion as to *why* it happened. Journalistic standards had always insisted on complete separation between news and editorial. That began changing. The lines became blurred. In the quest for more dollars, advertising techniques began to overrule many of the standards of journalists.

So, while remembering that the goal of advertising is to convince as many people as possible to buy your product, let's look at an exercise that I saw some time back. It's a very interesting and important exercise in how you can influence people. Since I will only be telling you about the exercise, I need to explain the second half first for it to make sense.

Picture a large lecture hall filled with a good many people. Everyone is divided into three groups, and they all have paper and pens. The group leader tells everyone that he wants to conduct a word experiment.

On a large screen he puts up a slide with the following letters: "H A _ E." He tells everyone that it is a four-letter word with the third letter missing. He then asks them to write down the word including filling in the blank for the missing letter.

When everyone has finished writing, he calls on the first group to reveal the word they wrote down. Every single one of them in the first group had written the word "HAZE." All the ones in the second and third groups looked confused. They didn't seem to understand how the first group could have come up with that word.

Then the group leader called on the second group to reveal what they had written. When they revealed their answers, every single one of them had written the word "HAVE." This time everyone in the first and third groups looked surprised and confused at the answer.

Finally, the third group was called to provide their answers. Again, all of them answered with the same word. It was "HATE." Like before, all the ones in the other two groups looked surprised at the answer.

So, why did the three groups give different answers, and why did all the members of the different groups give the same answer?

Let's now look at the first part of the exercise. The part that I left out earlier. Before the exercise began, the organizers decided that they wanted to try and create a situation where they could manipulate individuals in a group into providing them with predetermined answers. They did not want to tell the participants what they wanted, nor did they want to let them know of what they were doing.

All the ones in the first group were taken to a room with a large screen. They sat in chairs and put on headphones. They were told to select the type of music that they would like played through the headphones. The group leader then told them that they would be listening to music, but that they needed to pay close attention to what was on the screen. He said that they would be there about fifteen or so minutes.

Then the room then went dark, and the screen started showing three words over and over: "FOG" and then "MIST" and then "CLOUDS." When the fifteen minutes was up, the leader asked them if they knew the words shown to them. They were all able to recite the words from memory with no problem. All the ones in this first group filled in the missing letter with a "Z" making the word "HAZE." Can you see why they selected this word? It fell completely in line with the other words that had been placed firmly in the minds.

The ones in the second group were subjected to the same series of events, but they were given the words, "OWN" and then "POSSESS" and then "CONTROL." The ones in this group filled in the missing letter with a "V" making the word "HAVE" — have, own, possess and control.

Then the third group was set up exactly the same, but given the words, "REVULSION" and then "DISGUST" and then "DETEST." All the ones in this group filled in the missing letter with a "T" making the word "HATE." Can you see why?

None of the groups realized that they were being manipulated into providing a desired answer and all were genuinely confused and surprised by the answers given by the other groups.

None of the groups were wrong in any answer that they gave, and all of them were wholly convinced that their answer was the correct and logical one. All of them gave the answer by what was on their minds before the question was asked. They were conditioned to think in a certain way prior to being asked for their answer.

If you filled in the missing letter when the word was first shown here, then you gave the answer by what was in your own mind prior to your reading the rest of this paper. Again, there is no right or wrong answer, but we must realize that what we hear over and over again will impress and affect how we think.

If advertisers believe that the word *green* will help sales of whatever they are selling, then you will hear the word *green*, or you will see it, nearly every time you turn on your TV or read anything in the media. Constantly, you will hear and see the message that is desired to be given and received. We must realize that this is happening.

None of this is to suggest that every message is harmful, but most of these messages have less to do with your own best interest than they have to do with helping the ones sending the message. The messages sent do influence us, and we should understand how they work and that they do work.

The world is not wholly sinister, and these types of messages designed to condition people to do, or not do, things are not new. Many years ago, subliminal messages were sent out in department stores. You would hear music in the store but very softly and in a way that most everyone consciously ignored, were messages like, "Don't steal," "be honest," and the like. We do respond to being told things.

So, how does all this affect Freemasonry? Well, the fact is that Freemasonry has well-defined teachings and practices. These teachings are not changed by popular social opinion or advertising techniques.

But the problem is that some Masons may not be very familiar with the factual teachings of Freemasonry. This is because so very little teaching of Freemasonry has taken place in far too many lodges for far too many years. If someone has no base of reference or very little of a base, then they may just believe anything about anything when it is told to them again and again.

Politics and religion are two areas where Freemasonry has some clearly defined rules. Simply put, we don't tell our members as to which religious faith they should belong, nor to which political party they should belong. These are decisions that Masons need to make for themselves. Most jurisdictions even forbid discussions of religion or politics in open lodges.

But, in the new world of social media, I am seeing more Masons falling into one or the other of the hostile political camps born out of the new wave of information manipulation. Today our country is divided along political lines. I've seen unbelievably nasty political posts on social media on both sides of this political divide. I've seen Masons speak to Masons even in lodges in a way that not long ago would have resulted in charges of unMasonic conduct.

I should not have to say this, but Masons are entitled to believe anything they like regarding politics or religion, and we should never act unMasonic to our brothers because they hold different political opinions than us. Freemasonry teaches us better than this. We don't need outsiders getting into our heads and inciting us to take sides against our own Brothers.

It is one thing if advertisers try to influence us as to which soft drink or new car that we should buy. It is quite another thing when the harmony of Freemasonry is disturbed because brothers post hateful comments about other brothers in social media or even in lodges.

We need to see this for what it is and recognize that our teachings should put us above this attempted control from the outside. We *are* better than this, and we need to take complete control and govern ourselves accordingly.

But things are not all dark and dangerous with the media. Technology is providing us with some extremely useful tools that we can use in Masonic education. It is said that necessity is the mother of invention. It's true. This COVID-19 Pandemic has already provided us with some wonderful online platforms. Every time I turn around, I hear about, or am being invited to, some online education program by some lodge or other Masonic body. It is, without question, a dramatic shift in Masonic attitudes. I see real Masonic education happening time and again. I have no idea what will happen when this horrible time passes, but I am clearly seeing that humanity, as well as Freemasonry, is possibly heading to a new Golden Age that will follow this terrible time. I certainly hope so.

How Important is a Mason's Reputation?

Associate with men of good quality if you esteem your own reputation; for it is better to be alone than in bad company.
~ George Washington

We live in a world today where conflicting opinions are the norm. It's not always one opinion against another. It can be one opinion against ten different opinions, all spoken loudly, and with all the authority in the world. Social Media is filled with every imaginable view on every imaginable question. Actual, provable facts are often lost in a sea of *"I think."* Many times, in the area of reputation, the majority rules. Mass opinion often controls a reputation. If you plan to go to a restaurant but the reviews are mostly negative, then you will probably go somewhere else to eat. You don't know for a fact that the restaurant is below standards, but based on its reputation, you keep looking. Why take the chance?

A couple of years ago, I overheard two Masons talking about reputation. One of them said that since his reputation is decided by others, he never worries about having a good or a bad reputation. I thought about what he said. Because he seemed to be saying that we cannot control the thoughts or opinions of others, I somewhat agreed with him. But then I realized that everyone's reputation is important, and it does matter. Our reputation is created by what we say and do, or at least, what others understand of what we say or do. Our actions and words define what others believe of our nature. It is the perception that others have of us. It becomes who we are and what we stand for, at least, in the eyes of others. If we choose to live like a hermit, then maybe our reputation is not particularly important. But, if we live in society, then our reputation will determine how others view us and treat us. Yes, our reputation matters.

So, I have a question for you. When others think about you, what do they think? Of course, when I say "others," I don't mean the troublemakers, gossips, or those with any sort of axe to grind. I mean the average person, the one who has no reason to be unfair or lie to you or about you. What do they think of you? It's an important question.

I believe that one of the most difficult things to do is to try to get into anyone's head to understand what they think about anything. When you try to understand what anyone thinks or believes about *you*, it becomes a particularly personal matter, and the task becomes even more difficult. For that matter, what do we really think about ourselves?

Let's go outside of Masonry for a bit to maybe take a look at the situation from the outside.

Much of what we think about ourselves as well as others is almost hard-wired into our brains in ways that are often very difficult to understand. Many times, what we think of others is based on various clues and actions taken by them. We may not think as much as we just feel and believe. If we observe someone doing something, we judge it (and often instantly) based on preset patterns that our brain recognizes. We may not even be consciously aware of what we are doing. We may see something, evaluate it, and without thought reach a conclusion.

A while back I saw a documentary on hippopotamuses. It showed two big male hippos walking up to each other with a female watching over on the side. The two males were going to fight for the hand of the lady hippo. Slowly they approached each other and then they both opened their mouths wide. That was it. The fight was over. The one who opened his mouth the widest won. The one with the small mouth turned around and walked off. It is possible that the one with the smaller mouth was stronger, younger, fitter, and in every way imaginable a better match for the female. But something is wired in the brain of all hippos that the ones with the larger mouths are more dominate. The big mouth wins. That's it. That's how their brains are wired. It's how they see themselves and others. The one with the smaller mouth saw that the other had a larger mouth, and he felt that the other must be superior to him. The one with the larger mouth felt that he was the superior one simply because he had a bigger mouth. By that one action, they both believed something about themselves and the other.

But humans are a bit different. We can think and reason. We can question ourselves and observe results. How do we know that we can trust our readings or impressions of others? How do we know that insecurity or ego will not color how someone is evaluating us? We don't know. That's the problem. The hippo with the smaller mouth did not *know* that he was inferior, he just believed it. All he knew was that his mouth was not as large as the other hippo. Both acted in a way that was instinctive and their brains were wired to accept whatever result they observed. They didn't stop to analyze the result, they just moved on once the result was discovered.

Humans sometimes question and debate results. We may wonder if we had taken different actions if the results would differ. Or maybe the result means something different than what we first thought. We have calculating brains and we do have the ability to alter perceived results by changing the situations. Our intelligence can sometimes work in a way that can frustrate the daylights out of us. I believe that this is why we so often hear that our reputation does not matter. The task of trying to objectively understand how others think of us (with all the possible outcomes available) is too difficult. There are just too many options and situations that we can invent. So, we give up trying to understand it. We decide that it doesn't matter.

But in Freemasonry, does it matter that much as to what others think of us?

Here is the thing — being a Mason is something of having a dual-responsibility. Our actions reflect not only on ourselves, but on the whole of Freemasonry. It is because Freemasons have long held the reputation of being honest, pillars of society that when a Mason is seen as acting disreputable, it reflects on not just that Mason, but on all of Freemasonry. Fair or unfair, our actions do play a role in the reputation of Freemasonry. But again, if we are uncertain of how others are evaluating us, then how do we know anything about our actual reputation or how others see us? It is possible that we are hurting ourselves and the whole of Freemasonry without realizing it.

The problem we have is figuring out our own reputation. We want to determine if we need to adjust anything in how we act or things we say. We want to do this for ourselves as well as Masonry. Let's try to look at how we might be able to solve this problem.

While we might not know exactly how others view us, we can gain insight by taking a look at others. We can stand on the outside and watch the reaction and maybe even overhear comments about others to determine the other guy's reputation. The bottom line is that if someone has earned the reputation of being a jerk, study how they act and don't act that way! I know that this may sound like an oversimplification, but it really does have merit. Far too often, we need to take a good long look at ourselves, compare it with the words and actions of others, and be as honest as possible. It doesn't always have to be difficult. We all know a jerk when we see one. But, what about us? How are we seen? Are we sometimes trying to be funny, kidding around, and ... acting like a jerk? We have to be open to the fact that our actions or words may sometimes not be received as we intended. Of course, acting like a jerk doesn't mean that we are, in fact, a jerk. But we are talking about reputation, not reality. We are only talking about how others might view us based on their understanding of our words and actions.

While we have no ability to control the thoughts of others, we have total control over our own words and actions. If we step back and see that what we do or say might be giving us a reputation that we don't want, there are things that we can do to reverse a bad reputation. The first thing we need to do is be honest with ourselves. Is a bad reputation justified? If we can, without question, say that our reputation is not valid, then it will go away or not be accepted by those who know you. Fair people will not accept a bad, unjustified reputation. Those who may try to give a bad reputation usually die by their own sword. Their actions are eventually uncovered. They will be forced to answer for their damaging actions. But let's say that you did make some mistakes, and the reputation is fair, there are still things that you can do to turn things around.

If your bad reputation is based on things you are doing or have done in the past, stop it! Stop doing whatever it is that is giving you this bad reputation. Don't do it again. Sometimes you might feel that you are being misjudged or being given a bad rap for maybe only a small percentage of your actions, but most people unfortunately judge by what is memorable. Look at all your actions. Ask those close to you what might be a problem. If something you are doing can be a problem, it likely is a problem for some. Make note of it and try to change it. If you truly want to make changes in your life, and want a better reputation, you can and should make the needed changes.

It is not always ego that causes problems. Insecurity can create just as problematic a situation as an unchecked ego. We must all understand that everything we say and do affects others. We may feel that we are unimportant and that our actions or words have little effect on others, but it is just not true. What we say may not change some policy in a business or in Masonry, but people do hear us and evaluate us with every action and word we speak. None of us are invisible. Sometimes a bad reputation can even be created by saying things that we believe no one hears. We need to be attentive to everything we say or do. There is a balance that we need to achieve between not caring about, or being aware of, how we affect others and allowing others to control our actions. Finding that balance is a positive step toward rebuilding even a bad reputation.

Let's say that you only now learn that you have a less than stellar reputation within a certain group. You want to change that reputation. The time to act and begin work on changing things is now. Don't wait. We live in a social media world today when things happen quickly. Reputations can be destroyed in a matter of hours online. Acting quickly to repair a damaged reputation is essential.

Of course, not everything can be corrected at once, no matter how fast you act. Let's say that you have developed the reputation of being a smart-aleck. That's not how you want to be known. Yes, start now to correct that impression. Stop acting in the way that caused the problem. But you have to realize that it will take time for others to see and then to believe that this reputation is not valid. People will need to see you probably more than a few times to begin to reevaluate their opinion of you. But, having the reputation of being a smart-aleck, or silly, or even a jerk is one thing. There are other causes of a bad reputation that require other types of actions.

Maybe your reputation came because of something you said or did that hurt someone. Apologize. Give a sincere, meaningful apology. Make it clear that you messed up or acted badly. Fully own your mistake and make it crystal clear that you regret your error. Then, do not repeat the offense. This is the only way to begin to turn around a bad reputation earned by bad behavior. If you give only a half-hearted apology or attempt to make excuses for your actions to minimize your responsibility, then you have wasted your time. The apology will be seen as an attempt to avoid blame. Your reputation could be even further damaged.

Of course, make amends whenever it is possible. There are consequences for every action. If you, while playing around, tear a few pages out of an irreplaceable lodge Bible, you may not be able to undo the damage that you have created. But however possible make it clear that you regret your careless action. Sincerity and honest remorse can be felt and heard in our voices. Likewise, so can reluctant apologies or transparent excuses be seen for what they really are.

In times where something you have done has so crossed the line that there is no repairing the situation and making amends is not possible, accept what you have done. Regardless of if you do not view what you have done as all that serious, you need to accept the decision of the one wronged. Know when to stop. We must accept that sometimes the consequences of our actions result in situations that cannot be fixed. In such cases, the one wronged should have their wishes respected. Apologize, then give the desired space.

There are extreme cases where individuals such as burglars or drug dealers have gone to prison for their crimes, done their time, but they did not cease making amends once they were released. After their release, they spent the rest of their lives trying to repay society for their past actions by teaching kids the dangers of drugs or teaching classes on how to better protect your homes from burglars or con artists. We may never be able to overcome the facts of the past or our actions, but we can build new reputations and lives because of our actions from today forward.

This all brings us again to Freemasonry. What happens when we act badly in lodge or outside of lodge? What happens if we mess up and hurt not only our own reputations, but the reputation of Freemasonry itself?

One of the real dangers of a very good meal for me is the temptation to overeat. I do love good tasting food. Freemasonry has its own temptations. The countless degrees, offices, titles, and positions of power can be a powerful and highly attractive intoxication for too many. For those who have not attained much personal standing outside of Masonry, what is offered inside Masonry can be a great opportunity and help in their lives. Masonry can also be a very serious risk if one does not properly understand Masonic teachings.

If one in leadership damages his reputation, then not only do they also damage the reputation of Freemasonry, but they put a spotlight on that damage by virtue of their position of leadership. The damage to Freemasonry is far more serious than if the same event was with a Mason who was not in leadership. If one has any degree of leadership within Masonry and then has done something to cause disgrace to themselves and the Fraternity, then they need to make amends. They need to recognize the error (whatever it is), own up to it, and face the music. Once we accept any leadership position, then we *must* maintain a good personal reputation, as we become even more responsible for the Order's reputation than those who are not in leadership. We must all recognize the need to protect the reputation of Freemasonry, but those in leadership have a special responsibility. A problem for leaders is ego. Sometimes if a leader makes a mistake, ego will make him deny the existence of the error and compound the problem.

But what are the consequences for one in Masonic leadership turning out to be less than expected and developing a fair and earned bad reputation? For one thing, Freemasonry gets a very bad black eye. We will be saying to the world that we can, and do, put the undeserving into positions of leadership. Once that bell is rung, it cannot be unrung. But, Freemasonry has far more than one Mason in leadership, present and past. What is the responsibility of other Masonic leaders when one of their own damages the reputation of Freemasonry? How should they act? What should they do? Is this a problem they must deal with or is it OK to ignore it?

Let's look at a situation outside of Freemasonry that may be able to help us. Let's say that you are driving down the street and come to a corner where you stop. You notice three of your friends standing there, and they see you. They come running over asking you for a ride. You give it to them. As you are driving, you pass a bank. Your friends ask you to stop and wait for them while they go into the bank to get some cash. You pull over and watch as they go inside. Through the large window, you then see something very disturbing. They pull out guns and begin to rob the bank. What do you do? You think about driving off but decide to wait for them so that you can try to talk some sense into them. They jump in the car and yell for you to drive off. You start to leave but only get about a half a block when you are surrounded by police cars. It is clear what is going to happen to them, but what about you? You had no idea what your friends had in mind when you picked them up and then dropped them off at the bank. They didn't say a word to you about their plans. But you did see what they were doing in the bank, and you did wait for them then drive off in the car. It is very likely that you will be charged with the same crime as your friends.

Leaders in Freemasonry need to be very, very careful in any dealings with any other leaders who have done anything at all to harm the reputation of Freemasonry. If you even give the appearance of condoning or excusing bad behavior, then you could be painted with the same brush as them. Non-Masons will rightly see you as participating in activity just as problematic as the other leaders in trouble. *"For unto whomsoever much is given, of him shall be much required"* (Luke 12:48 KJV). If you have accepted any position of leadership, and you have received honors for it, then you owe something special to the Fraternity. If you allow "one of your own" to act in any way that brings disgrace to the Fraternity, then you will share in the consequences of his actions. Fair or unfair, that is the reality.

Freemasonry is taught by symbols. We must understand that the premise of teaching is that there is a teacher and a student. One of the major problems that I have seen in Masonry for far too long is that we are so often required to self-teach the important lessons and symbols. In the actual days of teaching Freemasonry (and I mean the philosophy and symbols, not ritual) there was always a teacher instructing several students. But those days are gone (for now). How do you teach yourself what you don't know? Sometimes it seems that we are in a locked room and the key to the lock is *outside* of the room. It is at times like these that we can turn to the teachings of Freemasonry. Masons should help each other. We should work in teams. We should use what's so often known as the "Buddy System." In Masonry, it is known as being our Brother's Keeper — always watching a brother's back while he watches yours. We must honestly and objectively watch each other — help each other. If you see your brother about to slip and do something that will damage his reputation, tell him. He will tell you if you slip. By working together, you can help each other avoid slips or repair damaged reputations.

In all things, recognize that Freemasonry is, and always has been, a progressive moral science. No one expects you to achieve perfection. It's not possible. Our goal is to always try to make daily advancements. One step after another. It may not seem like much, but it is harder than you might think. It is also more important than many think.

Balancing Masonry in Our Lives

In my opinion, one of the great problems that we, as human beings, face is falling out of balance — and that would be emotionally, spiritually, or physically. Whatever minor or serious problems are before us, it is easier to deal with them if we have balance in our lives. Likewise, small problems grow large and large problems become impossible if we are unable to ground ourselves or our emotions. I believe that whatever we are doing, we do it better if we are in balance.

So, what is balance?

In a nutshell, balance is when we remain in control of ourselves and our emotions. It is when we are in harmony with ourselves and things around us. It is when we have that inner feeling of peace.

We are in balance when we control ourselves and do not allow outside influences to create upset in us. Philosophers have written of the *Great Equilibrium* — the great balance between divine power and divine wisdom — between divine truth and law, between justice and mercy. It is this balance that is needed by all humanity no matter the religion or belief system.

In my experience, all of Masonry is a balance between what we should do and what we can do. Many times, we believe that the balance is between right and wrong, but I believe that sometimes this is too easy. The greater challenge could be to sometimes know when we must give up on something and move towards accomplishing something more attainable. Forever fighting for the unreachable is as out of balance as not knowing right from wrong.

Early in my Masonic career I was fascinated by the philosophy of Freemasonry. Then I reached a point when I became interested in Masonic history. It seems that I went through a phase when I felt that one could either pursue Masonic philosophy or Masonic history, but not both at the same time. This was a period when I was out of balance with myself and Freemasonry. It was only when I realized that the two merged into one that I felt that special comfortable feeling of knowing that I was on the right path.

The balance necessary for us as Freemasons comes from studying our early history, our ritual, the symbolism, and the unique procedures of lodge operation. The Mason in balance with Masonry understands all these aspects and recognizes in his heart, if he is true with himself, that he will always be as an Entered Apprentice — learning and growing.

It may be enough for some to have titles, degrees and powerful offices but is that really enough for us? Are these the sorts of things that will make us truly happy and satisfied? Does power, glory, and titles truly make someone happy? Does attaining these things leave us feeling empty? Does the more we get make us want even more?

Being in balance might mean focusing on ourselves and our own advancement, not concerning ourselves with what others are or are not doing. If we truly desire power, we might want to ask ourselves why. We might want to step outside of ourselves and ask why we have this desire. Is it to help others or ourselves? Sometimes taking a very good look at ourselves provides needed insight.

Some years back, I edited a book titled, *Masonic Enlightenment*. In that book, CC Hunt provides us with a paper titled, *The 47th Problem of Euclid*. In this paper, Bro. Hunt gives us a more symbolic understanding of this mathematical equation than is normally published. The great Pythagoras, it seems, was not the first one to realize the significance of this problem. The ancient Egyptians clearly understood this theory and made use of the triangle in many of their ancient structures.

But the symbolism of the *47th Problem of Euclid* is deeper than basic mathematics. The triad can be seen as the three principal officers of a lodge. We can also discover a way to use this equation to find balance. In his paper Brother Hunt tells us, *"Algebra is the application of symbols to mathematics, and Masonry is the application of symbolism in character building."* In this we find both the path and the goal. We find the balance within the teachings of Freemasonry.

The symbolic teachings of Freemasonry do provide us with the path for finding balance. The reason we would want to have this balance is so that we may have a better and more meaningful existence on Earth. That is the goal. We seek to be better than we are today and through Masonry we can find the means, if we try, to achieve our goals.

In some of the papers I've written, I've tried to take us back to the early days of Masonry. I've tried to go back prior to the days of Speculative Freemasonry and, as best as possible, look at the old Operative Freemasons. But I've also tried to go back much further than that and look at some of the philosophy that was used by ancient civilizations and compare those ancient philosophies with those of Freemasonry.

The goal was to try, as best as possible, to explore how things were done in much earlier and different times. I find value in studying how Freemasonry operated in times of war, in dealing with those who opposed us, and how we viewed ourselves and set ourselves up into organizations.

In looking at history, at least my take on it, it seems that the most difficult times for Freemasonry were those times when we appear to be out of balance. Freemasonry was never meant to be only a social club or a place to feed the egos of those who only desire rank, power, and authority. Freemasonry was always designed to be a place where through a specific method of teaching, we could improve ourselves.

Our ancient operative brothers did hard physical work. They used the time when they were not working to improve their minds and their manner of interacting with others. They did this with the goal of *being better*. Speculative Freemasonry took on the task of continuing the goal of making good men better. It was and is a sound blueprint for living.

When you take the symbolic teachings of Freemasonry and begin an examination of them one by one you find a profound educational system — a school. It is an education that is not found anywhere in the reading of lodge minutes or memorizing words with no effort to understand the meanings behind them. It is found by a systematic, regular, and serious study of each aspect of each of our degrees.

There are thoughts advanced by some that Masonry has run its course, or that the young men coming into Masonry are not truly interested in what we offer. But what do we offer? Is it that the new Masons are not interested in Freemasonry or not interested in the sometimes out of balance representation that we give of Freemasonry?

It is clear that we are in the middle of a time of great change. It is a change that is not only in the world but in Freemasonry itself. We are in the middle of a time that will require all of us to redefine not only ourselves but what we want and what we are willing to do to achieve what we want. I do not at all believe that Freemasonry, as an organization or philosophy, is coming to an end. I believe just the opposite.

What we have to offer, hidden away in dark, dusty areas on shelves almost lost, is exactly what is desired by more than a few. Our time of true purpose is near. I see one of the great problems of evaluating worth is the confusion between quality and quantity. Far too often we settle on mediocracy rather than make the effort to attain what is of real value. In too many cases, I see it believed that bigger must be better. I see it believed that we must not rock the boat. We must not try to change what has been around since before we joined. We are out of balance and fearful. We are doomed to failure and ultimate disappointment.

A few years back I drew criticism from some because I saw a photograph of a Masonic lodge in an obviously very poor corner of the West Indies. The altar was simply a plain wooden table with the Bible on it. At each of the officer stations was an old folding chair. About a dozen more beat-up folding chairs were around the sidelines. It was a sparse and plain lodge. The Masons milling around were obviously very poor and yet from their expressions, proud of their lodge. I drew the criticism because I said that I would rather be in such a lodge where real Masonry existed than in the most beautifully designed Masonic cathedral when none knew the true meaning of Freemasonry.

I do not believe that a lodge must be poor in order to understand Freemasonry. But I also do not believe that a large thriving and wealthy lodge necessarily understands the heart of Freemasonry. Simply being successful guarantees nothing.

There is a balance that we must achieve that has nothing to do with money, numbers, or success; it has to do with quality. It has to do with comprehending what we teach.

The moral philosophy of Freemasonry was not created by us but has been around, for all we know, since the beginning of mankind. While we still have war, hatred, and all the lesser qualities of humanity, we still hope to be better. We still have the way to become better. There is hope. I believe that this is why Freemasonry will not fade away. And even if it did, its teachings would come back with another name.

An interesting symbol of balance is the pendulum. Pull it too far in one direction and it becomes out of balance. Release it and it does not automatically come back into balance but goes out of balance in the other direction. Time is necessary for it to return to balance. But is that completely true? Is the pendulum the best symbol for balance? There is a thought that time and space exist only by our limited understanding of eternity. Maybe if we stop and wait to achieve balance then we may see that we achieved balance the moment we stopped. Of course, this is only a thought.

My parting hope is that if anything that I have ever written has given just one of you cause to stop and think about Masonry in a little different manner or has given you cause to dig a little deeper into any of these subjects, then I consider my work accomplished. I believe in planting seeds with the full knowledge that most of the seeds will not take. I'm good with that. Only one seed is necessary to grow a beautiful and powerful oak.

Peace be with you.

About The Author

Michael R. Poll (1954 - present) is the owner of Cornerstone Book Publishers and editor of the *Journal of The Masonic Society*. He is a Fellow and Past President of The Masonic Society, a Fellow of the Philalethes Society, a Fellow of the Maine Lodge of Research, Member of the Society of Blue Friars, and Full Member of the Texas Lodge of Research.

A New York Times Bestselling writer and publisher, he is a prolific writer, editor, and publisher of Masonic and esoteric books. He is also the host of the YouTube channel "New Orleans Scottish Rite College."

As time permits, he travels and speaks on the history of Freemasonry, with a particular focus on the early history of the Scottish Rite.

He was born in New Orleans, LA and lives a peaceful life with his wife and two sons.

More Masonic Books from Cornerstone

The Scottish Rite Papers
A Study of the Troubled History of the Louisiana and US Scottish Rite in the Early to Mid-1800s
by Michael R. Poll
6x9 Softcover 240 pages
ISBN 9781613423448

A Lodge at Labor
Freemasons and Masonry Today
by Michael R. Poll
6x9 Softcover 92 pages
ISBN 1613421834

An Encyclopedia of Freemasonry
by Albert Mackey
Revised by William J. Hughan and Edward L. Hawkins
Foreword by Michael R. Poll
8.5 x 11, Softcover 2 Volumes 960 pages
ISBN 1613422520

Measured Expectations
The Challenges of Today's Freemasonry
by Michael R. Poll
6×9 Softcover 180 pages
ISBN: 9781613422946

Seeking Light
The Esoteric Heart of Freemasonry
by Michael R. Poll
6×9 Softcover 156 pages
ISBN: 1613422571

Cornerstone Book Publishers
www.cornerstonepublishers.com

More Masonic Books from Cornerstone

A Masonic Evolution
The New World of Freemasonry
by Michael R. Poll
6x9 Softcover 176 pages
ISBN 9781613423158

10,000 Famous Freemasons
4 Vol. Softcover Edition
by William Denslow
Foreword by Harry S. Truman
Cornerstone Foreword by Michael R. Poll
8.5 x 11, Softcover 2 Volumes 1,515 pages
ISBN 1887560319

The Freemason's Monitor
by Thomas Smith Webb
6×9 Softcover 316 pages
ISBN: 1613422717

Ancient Manuscripts of the Freemasons
The Transformation from Operative to Speculative Freemasonry
Edited by Michael R. Poll
6×9 Softcover 190 pages
ISBN: 1934935603

Robert's Rules of Order: Masonic Edition
Revised by Michael R. Poll
6×9 Softcover 212 pages
ISBN: 1613422318

Cornerstone Book Publishers
www.cornerstonepublishers.com

New Orleans Scottish Rite College
www.youtube.com/c/NewOrleansScottishRiteCollege

Clear, Easy to Watch
Scottish Rite and Craft Lodge
Podcast & Video Education

www.ingramcontent.com/pod-product-compliance
Lightning Source LLC
LaVergne TN
LVHW091552060526
838200LV00036B/806